Experiment: Learning communities
edited by the Bauhaus Dessau Foundation
(Katja Klaus)

Schools of Departure No.

Article	Title/Author	Page
1	Progressive learning communities as an ongoing experiment Preface by Katja Klaus	49
2	Sim Van der Ryn and the 'Outlaw Builders' An essay by Greg Castillo	59
3	I love you in the name of the commons An essay by Binna Choi	71
4	Amereida: School, crossings and Open City Notes by Andrés Garcés Alzamora with Katherine Exss Cid, David Luza Cornejo, Rodrigo Saavedra Venegas	83
5	Inland—An academy for safeguarding seeds, animal breeds and knowledge An essay by Fernando Garcia Dory	91

Table of Contents

Article	Title/Author	Page
6	‘We are really fortunate to hold our sessions on the original BMC campus’ **Katja Klaus in conversation with Heidi Gruner**	103
7	Opening the academy: Oskar Hansen’s pedagogy of Open Form **An essay by Aleksandra Kędziorek**	121
8	Ant Farm—Show/Blow Minds (Learn) **An essay by Lee Stickells**	131
9	Biographies	145
10	Imprint	152

Table of Contents

Experiment: Learning communities

Outlaw Building News

75¢

making a place in the country

Spring 72

Cheap, lightweight,
quick
plastic bubble
with a view of the
bay
Not a house
more like a cradle
Doesn't sway much
even in the wind
but noisy and damp
when it rains
It's better-but. wetter
with no plastic,
as a place for
an afternoon nap

FOTO DOK
SPACE FOR DOCUMENTARY PHOTOGRAPHY
CasCo

Types of the Commons
cultural-knowledge commons
social commons
urban commons
natural commons
What to unlearn?
Rhythm

68
38
07
09
25
32
27

VIDA
amor

Revenge

SotA Radio 98.9 Fm
Any questions?
Ask me Michael
1 PetchaKucha
youtube playlist
MAYOR

CON
PETIT
FORME
1
4
5
E.T.C

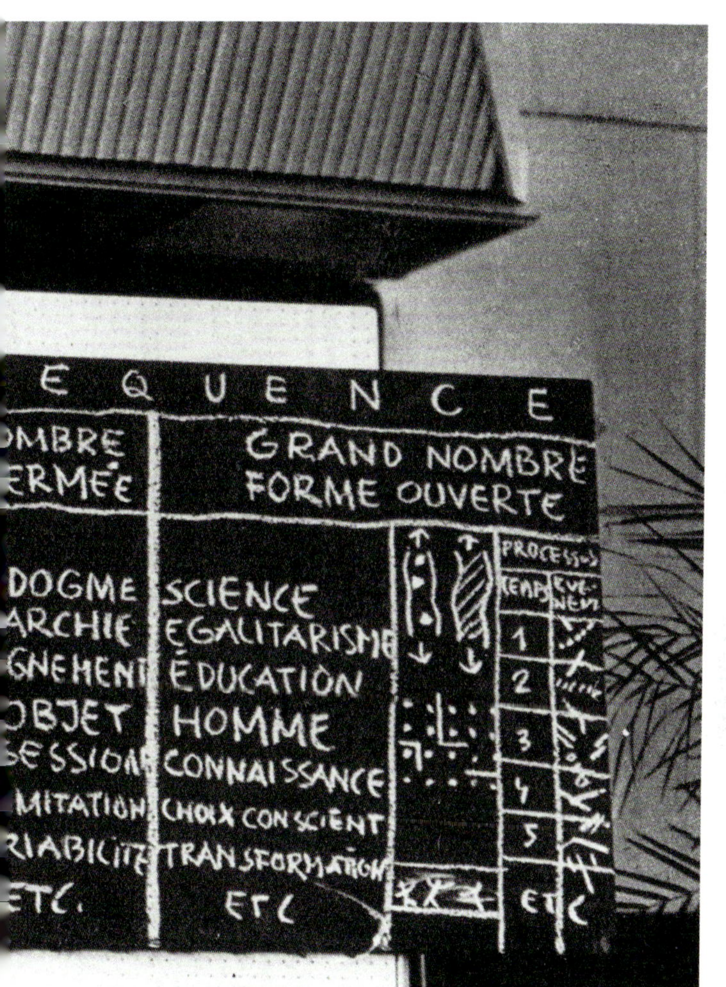

GRAND NOMBRE
FORME OUVERTE
DOGME
SCIENCE
EGALITARISME
ÉDUCATION
OBJET
HOMME
CONNAISSANCE
CHOIX CONSCIENT
TRANSFORMATION
ETC.
ETC
PROCESSUS
1
2
3
4
5
ETC

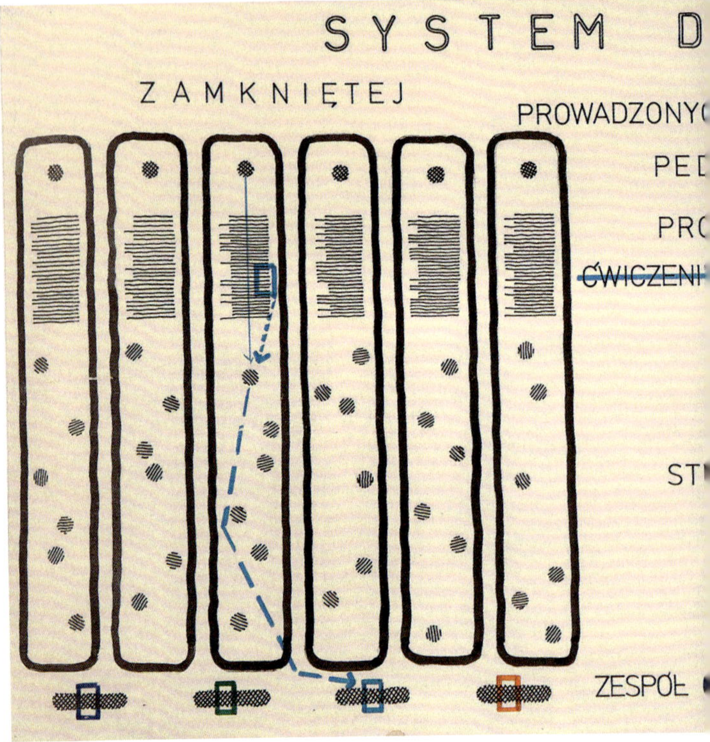

SYSTEM D
ZAMKNIĘTEJ
PROWADZONY
PE
PR
ĆWICZENI
ST
ZESPÓŁ

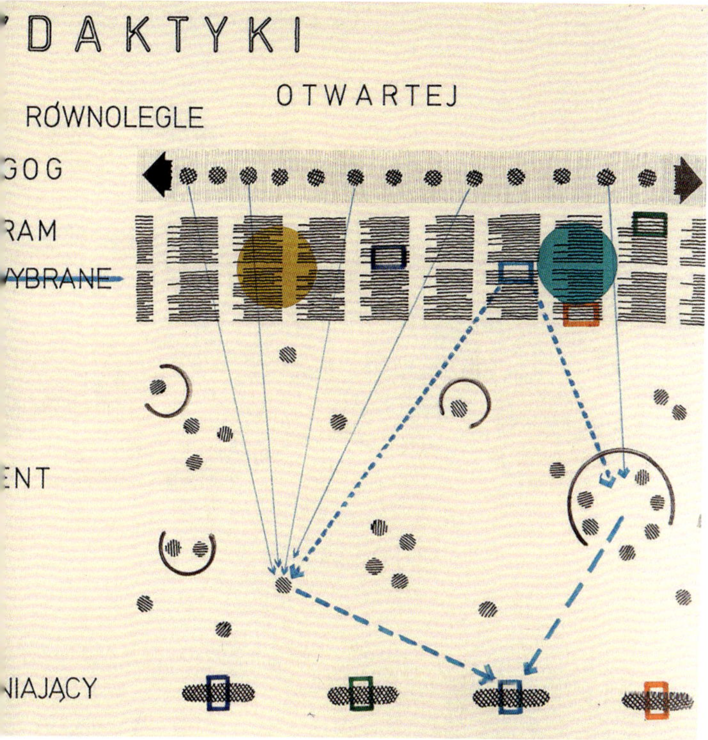

DAKTYKI

OTWARTEJ

RÓWNOLEGLE

GOG

RAM

YBRANE

ENT

NIAJĄCY

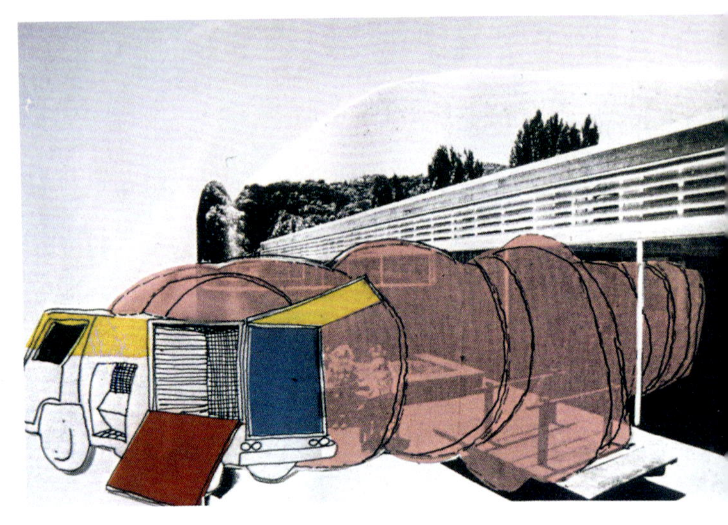

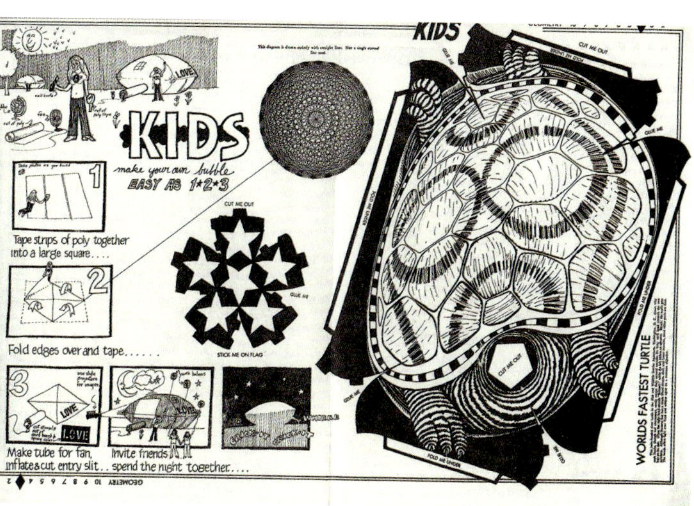
KIDS
make your own bubble
EASY AS 1*2*3
1
Tape strips of poly together into a large square....
2
Fold edges over and tape......
3
LOVE
Make tube for fan, inflate&cut entry slit..
Invite friends
spend the night together....
CUT ME OUT
GLUE ME
STICK ME ON FLAG
KIDS
CUT ME OUT
FOLD ME UNDER
GLUE ME
WORLDS FASTEST TURTLE
GEOMETRY 10 9 8 7 6 5 4 2

p. 6/7	Dismantling abandoned chicken sheds for old-growth redwood lumber to be used as a recycled building material. Photo: Jim Campe, Jim Campe document collection, Environmental Design Archives, University of California, Berkeley.
p. 8/9	The cover of *Outlaw Building News*, the final report generated by the students of Arch 102ABC, featuring a historical photo of a barn raising 'frolic'. Jim Campe document collection, Environmental Design Archives, University of California, Berkeley.
p. 10	Sim Van der Ryn lecturing at the 1970 International Design Conference in Aspen: montage of still frames from *Aspen 1970* (directed by Claudia Weill, Eliot Noyes).
p. 11	Berkeley's 'outlaw builders' constructing The Ark, a combination drafting room, dining hall and commons area. Photo: Jim Campe, Jim Campe document collection, Environmental Design Archives, University of California, Berkeley.
p. 12/13	Seven tables for Casco conceived by artists Falke Pisano and Riet Wijnen as part of their long-term plan to change the Casco's office environment, 2018. Photo: Angela Tellier.
p. 14	Casco team and Annette Krauss, Cleaning Together (with Mierle), 2014, a staged version of one of the exercises of *Site for Unlearning (Art Organization)*. Photo: Annette Krauss.
p. 15	Casco Art Institute's study lines (2018–2022) diagram by Binna Choi and David Bennewith, printed on fabric as part of Nina bell F. House Museum at Casco Art Institute, 2023. Photo: Chun Yao Lin.
p. 16/17	*The Courtship Tournament*, Jose Vial Amstrong historical archive.
p. 18	'Hospedería del Errante' in Ciudad Abierta. Photo: Andrés Garcés.
p. 19	Puerto Edén–Kawésqar Crossing, 2021. Photo: Andrés Garcés.
p. 20/21	Andrés Garcés Alzamora with Katherine Exss Cid, David Luza Cornejo, Rodrigo Saavedra Venegas.

p. 22/23
p. 24/25 Day 1 of Kate O'Connor's class 'One-Minute Grapefruit Strategies', 2019. Photo: Suz Sadler.

p. 26 Cheese ritual: Gathering of participants, 2022. Image courtesy of Inland.

p. 27 Zach Cooper's class 'Arriving at (experimental) Music' does a sonic meditation in a room-sized camera obscura, created by Sophie Bolla's class 'Parallax', 2017. Photo: Suz Sadler.

p. 28 Jonathan Curtin leading her class 'Queer Automative Theory'. Photo: Lauren Panichelli.

p. 29 During the very first session in 2017, participants set up a pirate radio station in the linen closet, and the radio kept going since at each session. Photo: Jordan Evans-Boyajian.

p. 30/31 Sky Dai & Eliah Eason's class 'Taking the Fall', 2019. Photo: Suz Sadler.

p. 32/33 Oskar Hansen, *To Trees and Birds*, 1994. Museum of Warsaw Academy of Fine Arts.

p. 34
p. 35
p. 36/37 Oskar Hansen at the AICA congress in Wrocław. Photo: S. Stepniewski. Museum of Warsaw Academy of Fine Arts.

p. 38/39 Oskar Hansen, a scheme of Closed Form and Open Form pedagogy, 1981, Museum of the Academy of Fine Arts in Warsaw.

p. 40 Farallones Designs, *Proposal for transforming a school, featuring the Farallones Institute's converted mail truck 'The Eagle' and inflatables*, 1969. Collage and ink drawing on paper. Private Collection. Image courtesy of Jim Campe.

p. 41 Ant Farm, *Inflatocookbook*, first edition (Kids, make your own bubble), 1970; offset printing on paper, two-sided; 11 × 17 in.; University of California, Berkeley Art Museum and Pacific Film Archive; purchase made possible through a bequest of Therese Bonney by exchange, a partial gift of Chip Lord and Curtis Schreier and gifts from an anonymous donor and Harrison Fraker.

p. 42/43	Ant Farm's *50 × 50' Pillow* installed at the Freestone Conference, 20–22 March 1970. Photo: Jim Campe; courtesy of Jim Campe.
p. 44	Ant Farm's *50 × 50' Pillow* installed at the Freestone Conference, 20–22 March 1970. Photo: Jim Campe; courtesy of Jim Campe.

Preface by Katja Klaus

Reading time 9′

Progressive learning communities as an ongoing experiment

1

The search for new communities, for ways of living
and working together, is experiencing a revival. Espe-
1 cially in times of crisis, people long more than ever for
collective forms of living, learning and working, for an
alternative way of organising life—in the present day
just as in the 1920s.

Collective action builds belief in new ways of life and models of society and gives rise to new spheres of action and thought. Commoning, a living process also defined as community building, has influenced the emergence of new communities in the 20th century and beyond. In community-based economic systems, communal gardens or alternative housing and education projects, people focused not only on fulfilling their own needs and jointly managing resources, but also on personal engagement and active collaboration, a connection with others.

At the same time, commons are not to be regarded primarily as resources or goods but rather as frameworks within social structures and processes. Silke Helfrich and David Bollier describe commons as models that generate satisfaction, which arise 'from a combination of personality, place, culture, time and political circumstance'. Commons, the authors add, 'prompt us to see the world from a fresh perspective and to fundamentally acknowledge that a self emerges from relationships and can only exist in and as a result of them. These "we's" are more than a sum of individuals. They come about in real and virtual encounters and in joint action.'[1]

Our society, the largest community we live in, is in
and of itself unstable. Anything is possible, anything
1 can change from one moment to the next. Covid-19, climate change, war, crises, personal freedoms, shared responsibilities—there was and is a huge amount to negotiate. The new communities are taking shape in the field of tension arising between open and closed, urban and rural, young and old, east and west, north and south. In this context, social inequality is driving us far apart, not only spatially, but also in terms of our experiences. We increasingly see the world from completely different perspectives and appear to be unwilling to engage with the other side. Especially in light of the diversity of the emergent digital communities, the question arises of how open we really are to different views or backgrounds and even whether we are merely operating in separate echo chambers, in which everyone agrees on the same things. Is commoning deteriorating here into an utterly naïve kind of wishful thinking, or is it perhaps even contributing to the romanticisation of present-day problems?

The content of the third edition of the e-journal in the digital atlas *Schools of Departure* is devoted to the diverse forms and dynamics of new communities in the field of design education. Learning communities focused on educational reform emerged in the early 20th century as a response to the inadequacy of traditional teaching methods given the challenges of the modern age and strove to completely overhaul both academic education and vocational training. This

issue examines not only a range of historic case studies, but also contemporary approaches to creating
1 alternative learning environments in art, architecture
and design.

How can new learning communities become successful, or what causes them to fail? The case of the historic Bauhaus sheds light on a central factor. These new communities are in most cases temporary projects. Collective ways of working are put to the test in the field of tension that exists between individual and collective creativity. When a new community is formed, its members mostly pursue a central idea, a concept and manifesto or at least a specific question. Ideally, theory and practice reinforce each other. The question 'How do we wish to live together and learn from each other now and in the future?' is accompanied by a practical commitment, namely, 'Who does not only think about the future, but is already trying out new things here, now?'

Who does not only think about the future,
but is already
trying out new things here, now?

At the historic Bauhaus as a community of people living, learning and working together, these questions
1 manifested themselves in the ambition of building for
a new society. The workshops as a framework for
training and production, the collaboration between
the different disciplines and training levels, and the
social connections between the members gave
shape for a limited time to a polymorphous learning
community. The existence and strength of the collective was rooted in key factors including an expedient
infrastructure, tried and tested practices, rituals and
celebrations, as well as a sense of belonging and a
spirit of social cohesion.

Who feels like they belong, and who belongs to the community? Essentially, there have always been people 'inside' and others 'outside', meaning that 'belonging' both includes and excludes people. The reasons for the failure of a learning community sometimes lie here, to which aspects such as the social climate, political pressure, fear of the new, hierarchies or financial dependency may be added too. The historic and contemporary case studies portrayed in the journal show the diversity of possible experiments, not so much as a recipe for a successful development of communities but rather as a testing ground for possible experimental orders.

In his essay, Greg Castillo introduces a course for architecture students at Berkeley University in 1970/71 which was committed to the countercultural agenda and was called 'Making a Place in the Country', also known as the Outlaw Builder Studio. Castillo

sees this as a critique of work practices in the professions of design and architecture and as an attack by
1 the counterculture movement on the traditional form
of architectural education. On this course, students and volunteers were invited to live and build on a forested hill north of San Fransisco. In the Outlaw Builder Studio, new forms of environmental analysis were combined with artisanal building methods and ethical questions of landscape conservation.

Based on the installation *To Trees and Birds*, Aleksandra Kędziorek presents the pedagogue Oskar Hansen and his endeavours to overcome the dictates of the Closed Form. Hansen, a professor at the Warsaw Fine Arts Academy from 1952 to 1983, instrumentalised his theory of Open Form to work against fully defined, dominant spaces. In the installation discussed here, he transformed a courtyard at the university into a backdrop for events. Throughout his life, Hansen focused on the development of non-hierarchical, absorbent spaces, on spaces for individual expression and on the integration and involvement of users in the design process.

Andrés Garcés Alzamora describes the Chilean school project Ciudad Abierta (Open City) as a poetic triad (life, work, study). Originating as an idea at the Universidad Politécnica de Cataluña, from the mid-1950s poets, architects and artists wrote the manifesto of the Open City Amereida (a composite of the words America and *Eneida*, Spanish for *Aeneid*) and on this basis established a place in which poetry and craftsmanship came together, a school in which poetry still has a place in the collective today.

1 The pedagogical experiments of Ant Farm in 1971 introduced by Lee Stickels in the journal likewise aspire to reshape architectural education through means of radical, alternative ways of living. In keeping with the ideals of the time, Ant Farm advocated the concept of learning as a 'continuous lifelong process' and the need to break away from traditional educational and professional institutions, spaces and modalities. Architectural teaching was to undergo radical reform, becoming an expanded sphere for situation-based learning incorporating happenings on the beach and other experiments in 'the art of life' according to their philosophy: everything from everyday life must be made magic.

For Heidi Gruner, the legendary Black Mountain campus in North Carolina is equally 'magic'. In the summer courses she initiated in 2016 in the School of the Alternative, the focus is on collective organisation, solid structures, community practices, methods of human conflict resolution, a radical world design and care of the community. Once a year, with her team she tries to create an ephemeral model of the world that everyone involved dreams of, without hoarding resources or gatekeeping knowledge.

The curator Binna Choi directed and guided collective transformative processes at the international Casco Art Institute in Utrecht. Under the additional title 'Working for the Commons', in recent years the institute has increasingly focused on the practicing and

sharing of common goods and on researching commons and their connections with art. To consistently
1 'unlearn' Casco's working methods in order to shape
the relationship to commons is absolutely essential,
not only for the institute's longstanding director, Binna
Choi. In her article she focuses on the transformation
process of this learning community, which has grown
over the past 33 years and continues to evolve from
a representational platform to a self-unlearning ecosystem for the art of commoning.

For Fernando Garcia Dory, unlearning the familiar, recognising the old and learning from the worldviews of smallholders and indigenous peoples, thus becoming open to new worlds of imagination, has become not only a creative exercise, but also a question of survival. Following his three-year experience at the Casco Art Institute, in 2009 he founded the agency Inland, which serves as a platform for diverse actors in agricultural, social and cultural production. The Inland project mobilises teams of artists in order to learn from rural communities and to lead a way of life that is connected to the land. They activate the rural environment with artistic tools such as mobile kitchens, radio stations or microarchitectures of farming. They engage with rural arts and crafts and in the process discover what must be changed at the core of art and design education.

1 Cf. Silke Helfrich, David Bollier and Heinrich-Böll-Stiftung (eds.). *Die Welt der Commons. Muster gemeinsamen Handelns.* Bielefeld: transcript, 2015, pp. 20 et seqq.

1

An essay by Greg Castillow

Reading time 13′

Sim Van der Ryn and the ‘Outlaw Builders’

Sim Van der Ryn's exploration of counterculture DIY building was personal and implicitly political. When shared through architecture school studio culture, it became pedagogical and professionally subversive as well.

In his foreword to the 1973 self-builder's publi-
2 cation *Handmade Houses: A Guide to the Woodbutcher's Art*, Sim Van der Ryn, a Berkeley professor of architecture, confessed the difficulty of mastering do-it-yourself (DIY) craftsmanship and asserted its importance as a means of mending divisions 'nurtured by the machine metaphor, by the separation of one's work from one's identity.'

'In 14 years of architectural practice I never designed a mortise and tenon joint because it was too much handwork and at carpenter's wages, far too expensive. Now I am learning to make them myself. It is taking me a long time to get over the guilt of spending days hard at work learning to do the things I wasn't trained to do. It is taking a long time to accept the simple satisfaction of doing what I am doing, living in the present.'[1]

In identifying itself as a licensed vocation, the architecture profession relies on the distance between its design practices and those of amateurs to maintain its occupational identity and social status. Professionalisation, as Gerry Beegan and Paul Atkinson point out, 'acts as a system of exclusion by setting up criteria that, intentionally or unintentionally, bar individuals and groups on the basis of money, class, ethnicity and gender.'[2]

Architecture training programmes and their licensing
examinations limit entry to the design profession and
reinforce professional norms and values. The system's inertia keeps change slow and manageable.
During the 1971–72 academic year at Berkeley's
College of Environmental Design, an elective studio
2 succeeded in circumventing those regulatory mecha-
nisms. Listed in the course catalogue as 'Arch
102ABC: Integrated Synthesis of the Design Determi-
nants of Architecture,' its counterculture agenda was
revealed in the two names by which the course was
more commonly known—'Making a Place in the
Country' and the 'Outlaw Builder Studio'.

Instructors Sim Van der Ryn and Jim Campe recruited students for a full academic year of research and construction on a forested hillside adjacent to the Point Reyes National Seashore in Marin County. Metaphorically, Arch 102ABC was a Trojan horse. Its 'on-site experience in the theory and practice of basic building design, land use, and village technology' injected the methods, ideals and building tasks of the hippie back-to-the-land movement into a professional design degree programme.[3]

Van der Ryn and Campe possessed ideal credentials to stage a fifth-column subversion of professional design pedagogy. Despite his 'disgruntlement with architecture school' as a student at the University of Michigan, hearing Buckminster Fuller lecture there sparked an 'epiphany'.[4] A second one came in the mid-1960s, around the time he accepted a teaching position at Berkeley. His participation in a clinical

2

The Outlaw Builder Studio fused new modes of ecological analysis with craft building methods and ethics of land custodianship.

study gauging the impact of LSD upon 'creatives'—a category that included scientists, engineers and designers—unlocked the doors of perception.[5]

When Berkeley students and hippies appropriated a block of vacant university-owned land in 1969 for the DIY commons called People's Park, Van der Ryn became fascinated with its 'spontaneous participatory design process' and then horrified by Governor Ronald Reagan's militarised response. Civilian gunshot injuries, the death of a bystander and the spectacle of a military helicopter spraying the campus with a virulent form of tear gas devised for use in Vietnam 'shook me awake', as Van der Ryn later recalled.[6]

Counterculture values suddenly permeated his teaching and design efforts. In 1970, Van der Ryn participated in two epochal design conclaves. He convened 'Freestone', an outdoor festival of hippie makers, 'to learn to design new social forms, new building forms that are in harmony with life'. Accompanied by a band
2 of eco-freaks bused to the Colorado using redirected university research funds, Van der Ryn disrupted the International Design Conference at Aspen.[7]

Joining forces with Jim Campe, an environmentalist and 'free school' reformer, Van der Ryn co-authored a DIY publication, the 1971 *Farallones Scrapbook*, dedicated to applying the lessons of hippie self-build methods to both schoolroom environments and childhood pedagogy.[8] Collaborating again to offer a Berkeley design studio, Van der Ryn and Campe mounted a counterculture assault on establishment design training—conducted, remarkably enough, from within an academic programme certified by the National Architectural Accrediting Board, an organisation created to regulate and reproduce the profession's standardised competencies.

The Outlaw Builder Studio fused new modes of ecological analysis with craft building methods and ethics of land custodianship. Morning workshops conducted on site imparted the know-how needed to establish a rural foothold, including 'adapting to the natural environment', site mapping, shelter design, tool use, carpentry and wood frame construction, and 'energy and waste systems'.

Guest lecturers provided additional instruction ‘in areas of knowledge or technique relevant to our interests’. The syllabus lists on-site talks on ‘Mobile Life Styles’ by members of the Ant Farm art commune; graphic documentation by Gordon Ashby, an alumnus of the Eames design office and a special issue
2 editor of the *Whole Earth Catalog*; material properties of wood by the sculptor J. B. Blunk; regional ecology by Gordon Onslow Ford, a former Paris surrealist and a disciple of the San Francisco Zen master Hodo Tobase; ecopsychology from wilderness-therapy advocate Robert Greenway, and ‘scrounging’ by Doug Hall, a member of the San Francisco T. R. Uthco artists’ collective.[9]

The variety of guests and breadth of their lectures convey the expanded field of counterculture design and its heady mix of empirical, spiritual and aesthetic enlightenment.

Acquiring building materials through scrounging rather than a cash transaction also proved transformative, imparting a new skill set that internalised abstract understandings of environmental sustainability. To make their ‘place in the country’, Berkeley architecture students scavenged old-growth redwood planks from chicken coops abandoned by the local poultry industry in its switch to factory farming.

By dismantling ramshackle sheds, scraping chicken shit from salvaged wood and trucking the hard-won gleanings back to camp, each student earned a new *nom de guerre*—‘Chickencoop Charlie’ being one example—celebrated with certificates enti-

2

'Making a Place in the Country' epitomised the kind of 'distribution of the sensible'.

tling holders 'to be known to all as an outlaw builder, with all the rights and privileges attached thereto'.[10] The 'outlaw' moniker was no joke: Nothing that the students built conformed to code requirements or had been granted a building permit.

Students constructed a DIY village around 'the Ark', a workshop and drafting studio that also served as a communal dining room. Surrounding it, personal sleeping cabins, a sauna, a cookhouse, an outdoor oven, collective shower facilities, a composting out-house and a self-composting chicken coop sprang up over the course of the academic year. At the end of the school year, Arch 102ABC students produced a jointly authored final report on the experimental stu-dio in the form of an underground publication, *Outlaw Building News*, that sold out as fast as it could be

printed. Assessing her hippie apprenticeship, a participant wrote: 'This ... was the first in 13 years of school where community and environment were not contradicted but constructed.'[11] It was a 'life architecture class', reflected another, an opportunity to 'build a house in which my physical self could exist and ...
2 a consciousness in which my spiritual self could exist.'[12]

The studio's idyllic setting and principles struck some as escapist: 'My social conscience tells me that I'm playing elitist games', commented another outlaw builder.[13] 'We share some belief in what we are doing as a way to learn about ourselves and about building', Van der Ryn reflected. 'We shared few explicit esthetics except perhaps a common regard for the land and a desire to use as many salvaged and native materials as possible.'[14] Mixing formal instruction in scrounging, DIY building, hippie nomadics and eco-metaphysics with a blithe disregard for zoning regulations and building codes, 'Making a Place in the Country' epitomised the kind of 'distribution of the sensible' associated with the concept of dissensus developed by philosopher Jacques Rancière.[15]

The rural studio organised by Van der Ryn and Campe advanced a foundational critique of work practices within the design and building professions. Although it remained untheorised in the text of *Outlaw Building News*, the proposal for an alternative ethos of architectural labour appeared on the front cover of the student publication. It features a historical photograph commemorating a barn raising, with women and children seen clustered at the base of the heavy timber frame and proud craftsmen waving hats and tools while balancing precariously above.

A voluntaristic building tradition now practiced primarily by Old Order Mennonite and Amish communities (and even there with ever-decreasing frequen-
2 cy), communal barn raising was widespread in
19th-century agrarian America when many hands were necessary to build a house and skilled tradesmen largely unavailable.

The most experienced neighbours led the crew, with others following their lead, learning to build in the process. Labour was rewarded not in cash, but through reciprocity: Participants knew that when they in turn needed to build, locals would rally to their aid. As a mode of communitarian work separate from the wage labour economy, barn raising also offered the pleasures of a social gathering. The Amish call this kind of work, which serves both sociable and practical ends, a 'frolic'—as apt a term as any for counterculture self-building pursuits. The outlaw builders' invocation of an Amish tradition can be dismissed, of course, as cultural misappropriation: a defamatory trope as common and as misleading as that of the 'lazy hippie'. Alternatively, retrieving a visual document of a self-build legacy that spurned commodified labour and proprietary skills can be seen in another way—as an attempt to identify a 'usable past', the term coined by the American literary critic Van Wyck Brooks to distinguish antecedent efforts capable of informing radical thought and action in the here and now.[16]

In their quest to define the communities of a sustainable society and their modes of 'right livelihood', counterculture self-builders ranged across time, evaluating archaic pasts and pharmacological futures for their utility as tools of resistance. Their records of achievement and DIY ideology are similarly available
2 to us today, should we ever need them for our own contemporary projects of self-reinvention.

1 Sim Van der Ryn, 'Preface', in: Art Boericke and Barry Shapiro, *Handmade Houses: A Guide to the Woodbutcher's Art*. San Francisco: Scrimshaw Press, 1973, unpaginated.

2 Gerry Beegan and Paul Atkinson, 'Professionalism, Amateurism and the Boundaries of Design', *Journal of Design History*, vol. 21, no. 4 (Winter 2008), p. 305.

3 Sim Van der Ryn and Jim Campe, 'Course Description' for Architecture 102ABC, Fall 1971, pp. 1–2.

4 Sim Van der Ryn, *Design for Life: The Architecture of Sim Van der Ryn*. Salt Lake City: Gibbs Smith, 2005, pp. 16–17.

5 Van der Ryn interviews with author, 2012–2014. The LSD testing programme at the International Institute for Advanced Studies in Menlo Park is discussed in John Markoff, *What the Dormouse Said: How the 60s Counterculture Shaped the Personal Computer Industry*. New York: Viking Penguin, 2005, pp. 58–65.

6 Van der Ryn, *Design for Life*, pp. 32–33.

7 'Advertisements for a Counter Culture', *Progressive Architecture* 51, no. 6 (June 1970), pp. 71–93; Greg Castillo, 'Counterculture Terroir: California's Hippie Enterprise Zone', in: Andrew Blauvelt (ed.), *Hippie Modernism: The Struggle for Utopia*. Minneapolis: Walker Art Center, 2015, pp. 87–101; Greg Castillo, 'Establishment Modernism and its Discontents: The IDCA in the

"Long Sixties"', in: Wim de Wit (ed.), *Design for the Corporate World: Creativity on the Line, 1950–1975*. London: Lund Humphreys, 2017, pp. 41–59.

8 Farallones Design, *Farallones Scrapbook: Making places, changing spaces, in schools, at home, and within ourselves*. Farallones Design: Pt. Reyes Station, CA, 1971.

9 Van der Ryn and Campe, 'Course Description', p. 5.

10 Van der Ryn, *Design for Life*, p. 40.

11 Terri Martin, quoted in Sim Van der Ryn et al., 'Inventory', *Outlaw Building News* (1972), n. p.

12 Anonymous, quoted in Sim Van der Ryn et al., 'Inventory', *Outlaw Building News* (1972), n. p.

13 Gail Morrison, quoted in Sim Van der Ryn et al., 'Inventory', *Outlaw Building News* (1972), n. p.

14 Sim Van der Ryn, quoted in Sim Van der Ryn et al., 'Inventory', *Outlaw Building News* (1972), n. p.

15 Jacques Rancière, *Dissensus: On Politics and Aesthetics*. New York: Continuum, 2010.

16 Van Wyck Brooks, 'On Creating a Usable Past', *The Dial* (April 11, 1918), pp. 337–41; Alan Trachtenberg, 'Mumford in the Twenties: The Historian as Artist', *Salmagundi* 49 (Summer 1980), pp. 29–42.

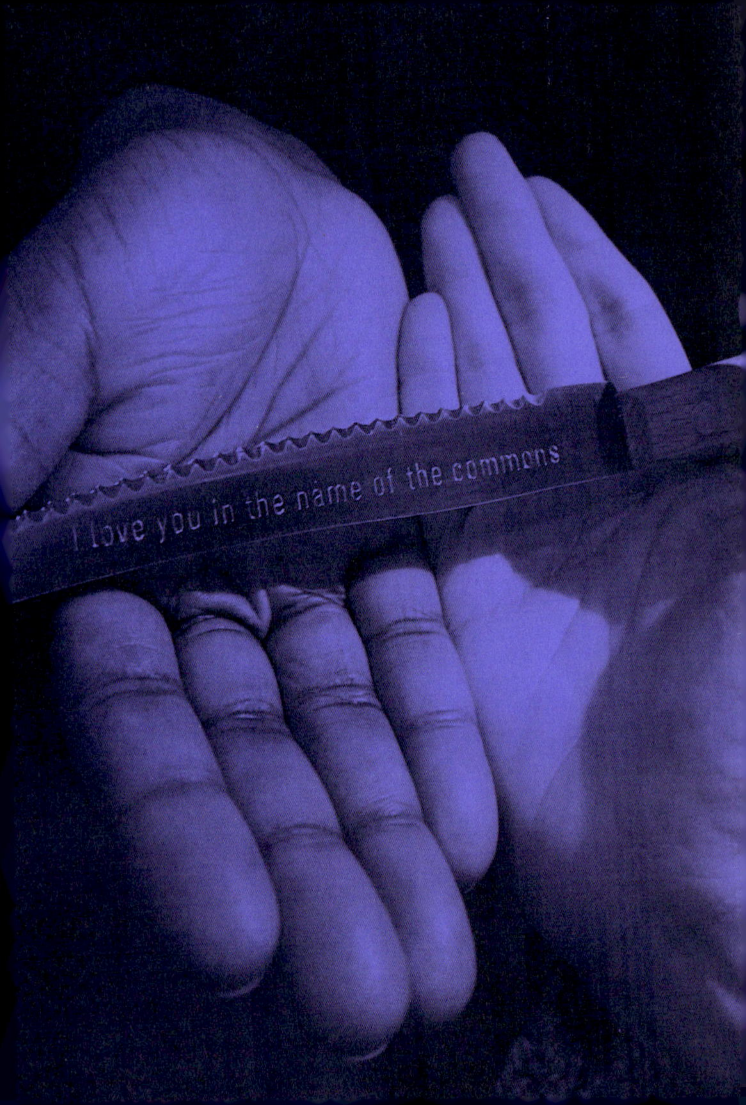
I love you in the name of the commons

Notes by Binna Choi

Reading time 12′

I love you in the name of the commons

1
IMAGINING AN ART INSTITUTION AS A TREE

Imagining an art institution as a tree allows us to
think of growth in a different way from what colonial
capitalism compelled us to do, namely in terms of
expansion, extraction, exploitation and profits. The
so-called edifice complex is coupled with museums
that, as a meme says, 'are designed to preserve the
inert and exclude the living'. Even though the (art)
objects in museums are not as inert as we think and
3 the simple binary of the dead in contrast to the living
may no longer be valid, most museum protocols point
at the opposite. What would an art museum be like if
it were a tree?

Let us imagine a forest of small to mid-size art institutions that sprung up in the 1990s across the globe—that is 'in the era of globalization'—unlike the 19th-century bourgeois or state model art institutions like museums with collections. The Casco Art Institute has been growing for 33 years now. First it was meant to fill a gap and be a public platform for presenting works by artists from the city of Utrecht and elsewhere in the Netherlands. After about five years it evolved into treating its space as a multi-functional studio for research, experimentation, production, discussion and presentation while going out into the 'public' space and working with artists from other parts of Europe.

This made Casco known as Casco Projects, as the domain of the Casco website was called at the time when the Internet became part of everyday life. The director at that time, Lisette Smits, told me once that *Deschooling Society* (1971) by Ivan Illich was her bible for directing the institution, which actually has to do with deinstitutionalisation of both art and education or even beyond that of living and being.

The following directors, Emily Pethick and myself, did not digress from that but joined the pursuit of this cause with different strategies, methods and practices. As a strategic move to articulate its position within the Dutch contemporary art and cultural land-
3 scape, the Casco team and board added a new subtitle to Casco, calling it Casco, Office for Art, Design and Theory. During the time of receiving this name, Casco enhanced the focus on an interdisciplinary and participatory approach in art practice. The languages of graphic or architectural design were tested, and their experimental forms offered a support structure as well as spatial or literary expression to what Casco and artists do.

The following phase up until now has been marked by another change in the institution's name into Casco Art Institute: Working for the Commons. Guided by the process of researching the notion of the commons and how art is related to that with a number of artists, local students and neighbours, the Casco team and artist Annette Krauss took on the process of unlearning Casco's way of working in order to shape its relationship with the commons.

This process coincided with Casco engaging with the self-transformative process of the Arts Col-

laboratory network consisting of similar kinds of art institutions, which, however, were located in the so-called Global South, and soon after that with the agro-ecological history of Leidsche Rijn, a newly urbanised area of Utrecht with the Outsiders collective. In other words, the institution's own journey of decolonising its scope and mode of working slowly led it to be open, wide and rich in its relationality with 'others' or rather 'one another' as you move away from assuming the world is organised around the principle of 'us versus the others' but within a forest of trees, as
3 one could say.

Recently Casco made a public announcement about its 'ecosystemic shift', which suggests a new mode of governance and economy in a commoning institution. We are going to see how this will evolve again, especially as our ecosystem at large on a planetary level is going through the drastic if not catastrophic change.

2
A DESK OF ONE'S OWN

While there can be no commons without a community that takes care of and benefits from the commons together, this does not mean there has to be a collective or collectivity in all aspects and all the time. In fact, in shifting to Casco Art Institute: Working for the Commons—from a mode of representing to a mode of practicing and sharing the commons—more attention was given to each individual in the team as symbolised by the replacement of a big collective office table by several individually customised desks in different sizes.

In a hierarchal structure governed by the public or private rule, power is centred on a few selected individuals in management and the rest of the team are subjected to the decisions made by them and somehow remain replaceable as per their functions. As a team making a transition from a public or private body to the commons, that meant for us that each person is ensured of her, his or their own subjectivity as a practitioner of the commons, and we hold on to an
3 awareness and responsible acts that imply we are taking care of the institution together.

This assurance was made through how each person feels connected and committed to what we called study lines, each of which includes a wider community of shared concerns. The notion of study was inspired by Fred Moten and Stephano Harney[1] as a way of learning and living by acting and planning together in resistance to oppression, indebted to the anti-slavery struggles, and if possible with the sense of prophecy of what is to come. The 'study lines' refer to the key areas of commoning in our own terms.

The team indeed has been changing in this regard, and it's important that no team remains the same, and this aspect of individual transformation along with a collective transformation has to extend beyond the team, involving collaborators and co-learners while the boundary between the team and the ecosystem dissolves, facilitating movement and on-going reconfiguration in the ecosystem. In the commons, I believe, everyone has to be a leader who knows which person or thing should take their turn of leadership and who knows how and when to act as an assistant. This goes against the undiscriminating idea of a flat horizontalism and its tyranny.

Of course there is already a deep sense of caution of a mob when different scales of the commons are imagined, let alone gated communities and other enclosures. Still, we need to see stars, be stars, and stars are together and far away to make up the universe. Last but not least, at the same time, the pre-
3 condition for this kind of leadership should be that it has its foot down on earth, for which 'cleaning' could stand as a synecdoche.

3
CLEANING HABIT FOR THE COMMONS

Cleaning our office together is one of many exercises that the Casco team and Annette Krauss tried as a strategy of unlearning our anxiety-driven busyness, which stems from our habitual desire for productivity and expanding, competitive business. While some exercises like 'reading together', 'mood colour' or 'property relations'[2] were tried once, others, like cleaning, have been made into the ritual and habit. It is significant in many ways.

One is the recognition of perpetual inequality in gender and race as we can see people originating from the former colonies come and clean homes and offices in the countries of the colonisers. In the devel-

oped world, still many more women or especially women of colour than any men babysit and cook for children, especially away from their own home. This has to do with how coloniality persists in the modality of capitalism and how it perpetuates to undervalue the realm of reproductive labour or rather depends on its being cheap or free labour, all the while separating the productive and the reproductive, and making the latter invisible. This can be seen in the self-(re)producing natural ecosystem as well. The labour of nature is completely ignored. Nature is only seen as a
3 source for exploitation and extraction which has been leading our time to being an era of mass extinction.

In the way the question 'Who cleans the world?' led Françoise Verges[3] to examine decolonial feminist struggles in critiquing white-women-centred feminism, the act of cleaning together led us to examine different domains of reproductive labour and to seek the possibility of undoing the separation of production and reproduction. Faisol Iskandar, a leader of the migrant domestic workers' movement in the Netherlands, has told us and above all showed us how cleaning defines what leadership should be about. It's not about resting in an armchair while someone else is cleaning for you. It is cleaning, cooking, taking care of people to support life in your community and wider ecosystem.

'The commons provide services which are often taken for granted by their users: those who benefit from the commons do not take into account their intrinsic value, only acknowledging it once the commons are destroyed and substitutes need to be found. To some extent, the universal services provided by the commons are similar to household work, never noticed when the work is being done. Only when no one is there to do the dishes, you notice its value.

In other words you don't miss something until it is gone. Two striking examples of this feature are represented by mangroves and by coral barriers: people living on the coasts are not able to estimate the value of the services they provide simply because
3 they don't even know that these goods have a specific function, that they are doing something for them. Only when a Tsunami hits, destroying villages, the value of such vegetation becomes apparent. However, prior to their destruction, mangroves played a major role in protecting coastal villages from tsunami waves. It would be highly expensive to build a similar barrier artificially.'[4]

4
IN THE NAME OF NINA

The figure of Nina bell F. was conceived around 2016 by former team members, artists and cultural practitioners at Casco Art Institute out of a shared concern to care for and maintain the ongoing practice of commoning and to unlearn current practices with the aid of art beyond oppressive institutional boundaries and habits. Their/her name conjures up the artistic, Black, feminist and political engagements of Nina Simone, bell hooks and Silvia Federici. As Nina continues to live, the practices of many others are called upon, keeping her/them as a collective figuration that transcends individual personhood and institution/organisation as well as the ordinary divisions of artwork, labour and life.

The House Museum was created to manifest the embodiment of Nina, offering the public a way to recognise and possibly be part of Nina. The Nina bell F. House Museum collects and shares ephemera, leftover objects, notes, snapshots, among other (accidental yet telling) things unearthed from the archives
3 of the Casco Art Institute's exhibitions, projects and collaborations each of which tells the story of Nina.

It foregrounds the non-conventional practices of archiving at the heart of small institutions which often remain invisible, undervalued and overlooked due to the culture of visibility and the accelerative and extractive modus operandi prevailing in our time. Simultaneously, the House Museum works at odds with other institutionalised archival practices that tend to hoard, guard and stall archives by insisting on forms of openness, vitality and deliberation where the collection is made accessible for use, contribution, co-creation, exchange and circulation over time.

The museum itself may be small, but it is potentially ubiqultous, it may look static but it keeps on breeding different beings who find a way of living together and transforming together. A series of small 'fermentation houses' as the House Museum's architecture were provided by Amsterdam-based artist Donghwan Kam. They indicate that the dwelling place of Nina exists beyond the visible and physical realm while sheltering and making a new alchemy to be collectively tasted.

1 Fred Moten and Stefano Harney, *The Undercommons: Fugitive Planning & Black Study,* Minor Compositions, 2013.

2 For more information on the unlearning exercises, please refer to Valiz with Casco Art Institute: Working for the Commons. *Unlearning Exercises: Art Organization as Sites for Unlearning,* 2018, https://casco.art/resource/unlearningexercises/

3 Françoise Vergès, *A Decolonial Feminism*, London: Pluto Press, 2021 (the original French edi-
3 tion was published in 2019).

4 Ugo Mattei. *The State, the Market, and Some Preliminary Questions about the Commons* (French and English version), University of Turin and IUC Research Commons, 2011; http://ideas.iuctorino.it/RePEc/iuc-rpaper/1-11_Mattei.pdf

Notes by Andrés Garcés Alzamora with Katherine Exss Cid, David Luza Cornejo, Rodrigo Saavedra Venegas

Reading time 13′

Amereida: School, crossings and Open City

4

The Escuela de Arquitectura y Diseño (School of Architecture and Design) at the Pontifical Catholic University of Valparaíso, Chile, has based its work on the relationship between the trades or crafts of architecture and design, and poetry. This has resulted in the construction of a vision that has been sustained for some 70 years now, in which the steps leading to an understanding of architecture and design are connected to an aural experience of the poetic word.

THE QUESTION OF BEING AMERICAN

Since the school's founding in 1952, this relationship
between poetry and the practices of architecture and
design has enabled the development of a complex
and reflective look at the intimate singularity of being
4 American and the American's relationship with the
world. In 1965, this gave rise to the first *Travesía*
(crossing), a poetic journey across the South American continent from Tierra del Fuego, Chile, to Santa
Cruz de la Sierra, Bolivia, which was taken by the
founders of the school and a group of artists, philoso-
phers, poets and sculptors from different countries.
Based on this experience they wrote the visionary
poem *Amereida*, inspired by Virgil's *Aeneid* and the
explorer Amerigo Vespucci. The poem was written in
1967 and led the group to founding the Ciudad Abierta, the Open City, in 1971.

Amereida evokes the star constellation commonly known as the Southern Cross, the cardinal points of which stand for the origins of America in the Caribbean, the adventure of the Pacific Ocean, an anchor at the South Pole, and the light of the Atlantic Ocean. Within the star constellation, the axes of 'our own north' are traced and the relationships that enable us to understand the continent from an original perspective are identified. The *Travesía* questions the European tradition, 'the ancient theft', of the inland sea of America—as the inland territories of America are called in the poem *Amereida—*, the Pacific Ocean and present-day life on this continent populated by aboriginals, mestizos and immigrants—by going out to explore America every year from 1984 to the present day. This has meant having the attitude and the will to step up to whatever occurs in American life.

OBSERVATION

4 At the School of Architecture and Design, observation is one of the fundamental tools resulting from the link between craft and poetry; it challenges students and teachers to know and understand reality. Observation is studied in an intuitive and profound practice of inquiring into reality which is reflected through the sketch as an abstract freehand drawing or named through a written annotation that describes the qualities and intangible relationships of the place. It is invariably a question of unveiling human acts and their positioning in space.

CIUDAD ABIERTA—OPEN CITY

The Open City was founded in 1971 in a collective act among sand dunes, marshland and low hills on the south-eastern coast of the Pacific Ocean, west of

Mount Aconcagua and close to the city of Valparaíso. In the context of his active participation in the Chilean university reform of 1967 and the global clamour of wanting to 'change the world', the poet Godofredo Iommi, the founder of the school, invited us to reorient the university and open up the possibility of realising this as an ideal space where life, work and study come together in unison. This signified a tremendous adventure entailing new ways of living, both personally and collectively. The poetic triad (life, work, study) became the horizon of the founding of the Ciudad Abierta, giving it the gift of being the meeting place between poetry and craft in the light of the poem *Amereida*.

It has meant more than fifty years of permanent
4 work, focused on human habitation, giving tangible form to the act of 'hospitality' in the sense of 'hearing the other for what he or she he is'.

In the Open City, students, teachers and the community come together, interacting creatively in pedagogical and artistic fields in close relationship with the natural space that makes up this territory. They give meaning to living in unison with this medium where the work is placed in the light of the poetic word that gives meaning to life.

Since the school's foundation, its students have participated in creating the works of the Open City through research projects that materialise in works of architecture, design, sculpture and other visual arts, promoting a constant reflection regarding the living conditions of the human being.

POETRY IN ACTION

In the arenas of the Ciudad Abierta, life revolves around the idea of 'the return to not knowing' (various authors, 1971), meaning suspending or moving away from certainties, from what is justified by the habits accumulated in life. The poets have been part of this collective from the beginnings to the present day, contributing—with their unique way of seeing life—to all the activities of the School of Architecture and Design and the Ciudad Abierta.

They propose the poetic act as a celebration in the form of a game that, in ordinary and colloquial language, finds a key that allows us to recognise the singular, that which is proper and constitutive of that place (Reyes, 2016), in the encounter with the people
4 who participate in the act, configuring their 'here and now'.

THE PLAYFULNESS OF HABIT

The 'playfulness of habit' explores the forms and daily acts of the human being in order to decipher their true meaning through observation. From this origin, their divergent and playful expressions that enable human creativity are explored. This seeks to go beyond function as a utilitarian origin of objects to delve into the mystery of forms as a cultural and transcendent form of expression (Lang). The 'playfulness of habit' relates human acts and artefacts to the disciplines of design and architecture through the multiple celebrations, competitions and exhibitions that have taken place throughout the history of this school.

> It is necessary to obey the poetic act, with and despite the world, to unleash the 'fiesta'. And the 'fiesta' is the game, the mandatory provision of my freedom. Such is the mission of the poet, because the world must always be passionate. (Godofredo Iommi, 1971)

ALWAYS THE SAME,
4 NEVER THE SAME

We live in the re-creation of the present understood as a gift. This way of thinking leads to the daily construction of a common sphere of life in the eagerness to exhibit everything that has been made collectively, in which the collective nature of the creative act is preemptive through the different workshops that take place in the School of Architecture and Design and in the Ciudad Abierta.

In the *Travesías* and in the Open City, the contemplative action of observation is linked to the practical action of building and the poetic action of giving. And it is in the relationship of these three dimensions that the educational model of our School of Architecture and Design is structured.

Bibliography

Corporación Cultural Amereida. http://amereida.cl/Ciudad_Abierta

Iommi, G. (1971). *Carta del errante;* https://wiki.ead.pucv.cl/Carta_del_Errante

Iommi, G. (1971). *Voto Propuesto al Senado Académico 1969;* https://wiki.ead.pucv.cl/Voto_Propuesto_al_Senado_Acad%C3%A9mico_1969

Iommi, G. et al. (1967). *Amereida, Volume I,* edited cooperatively by Lambda (https://wiki.ead.pucv.cl/Amereida) and the Escuela de Arquitectura y Diseño de la Pontificia Universidad Católica de Valparaíso, Chile (https://www.ead.pucv.cl)

Lang, R. *Taller de la diversión del hábito.* https://wiki.ead.pucv.cl/Taller_de_la_
4 Diversi%C3%B3n_del_H%C3%A1bito

Reyes, J. (2016). *Atajo de Amereida;* https://wiki.ead.pucv.cl/El_atajo_de_amereida

Travesías de Amereida; https://www.ead.pucv.cl/experiencia/travesias/

Various authors (1971). *Apertura de terrenos;* https://www.ead.pucv.cl/1971/apertura-de-los-terrenos/

An essay by Fernando Garcia Dory

Reading time 15′

Inland— An academy for safeguarding seeds, animal breeds and knowledge

5

The virtual space that this issue of the e-journal creates invites readers to think about education as part of a conceptual process and an aesthetic operation in the arts. This is especially important at this moment of uncertainty and growing pressure to transition towards another paradigm of civilisation, involving not only important economic and technical changes, but also a transformation at the very core of the productive model, values and culture.

For three years, I worked with Casco in the Netherlands, a relatively small arts organisation with a very strong propositive and experimental capacity that has long questioned many aspects of the art system and looked at its political economy. From that time, I remember a strong concept central to our joint programme concerning the commons, post-Fordist cultural working conditions or feminist economies in Casco's research. At the same time, I developed the Inland project. The concept centred on 'un-learning'. This idea contains many central aspects of the chal-
5 lenges we are facing, among them environmental or social justice struggles.

Un-learning many aspects of the techno-scientific rationality, European anthropocentrism and the faith in economic growth at any cost has become a matter of survival. To un-learn, to recognise—from the Latin *re-conoscere*, to know again—is to a certain degree a creative exercise and means not only to learn from other subaltern realities such as the peasant and indigenous cosmovisions but also to build upon them, allowing new imaginaries.

Is it maybe in that sense that Friedrich Schiller's *On the Aesthetic Education of Man in a Series of Letters* (1795) connected art appreciation and beauty with a set of values. That intention guided different artists to develop projects that went beyond the individual sphere of creation or even beyond what would be considered art in their time. John Ruskin devoted himself to an active critique of the early days of industrial capitalism by defending a form of arts and crafts for the enhancement—also morally—of the everyday. He also promoted different educational initiatives, such a Migratory Dairy School to extend new cheese making techniques amongst farmers as a way to increase their incomes and thus keep the rural areas alive. Another important project he engaged with was the Coniston Mechanics' Institute, which was established in 1852 to promote lifelong learning and continuing personal development for the workers of Coniston. At that time, the local population was around 1,300, with some 600 employed in copper mines.
5 Without their own building, classes such as woodcarving and lectures on topics like geology, art and local history would take place in the village school located in St Andrew's Churchyard.

In 19th century Britain, there were well over 700 Mechanics' Institutes. They were created by industrialists and philanthropists to educate the emerging industrial society in the new technologies of the age. Whilst on the one hand they were clearly instrumental, designed to create a more productive, healthy and enterprising nation of workers, they were also

Many important educational initiatives under the umbrella of the Institute for Free Teaching

altruistic, offering a broader education in the arts and a place for social gatherings—albeit to steer the people away from the public house. Subsequently, such institutes became the seedbed of social reorganisation, democracy, women's rights, co-operatives, friendly societies and unionisation. With the passing of the Public Libraries Act in 1850, many of these institutes became public libraries or universities (for instance in Manchester, Leeds and London).

During the same period, Russian writer Leo Tolstoy established on his estate the school Yasnaya Polyana for peasant children, in which different innovative pedagogical initiatives were brought to life. In his own words, 'The school had a free development based on principles established in it by teacher and pupils. Notwithstanding all the weight of the master's authority, the pupil always had the right not to attend the school and not to obey the teacher.'

In 1921, Indian poet and philosopher Rabindranath Tagore bought a large manor house with surrounding land in West Bengal where he set up the Institute of Rural Reconstruction that came to be known as Sriniketan after its location. The school Silpa Bhavana in close-by Santiniketan had already started providing training in handicrafts. Sriniketan took over the work with the objective of bringing back life in its completeness to the villages and to help people to solve their own problems instead of having solutions imposed on them from outside. An emphasis was laid on a scientific study of the village's problem before a solution was attempted.

In line with such ideas about the reconstruction of village life, a new type of school was also conceived, intended mainly for the children of neighbouring villages, who would eventually offer up their acquired knowledge for the welfare of the village community. This promoted forms of non-formal education among those who had no access to the usual educational opportunities. It continued in the 1930s with a training programme for village school teachers. An agricultural college was established in Sriniketan, and even a rural research centre was set up in the 1970s.

In Spain in 1911, in the context of the new Republic's impulse for regeneration—in a divergent thread of history that in some ways now looks like a lost opportunity—many important educational initiatives were launched under the umbrella of the Institute for Free Teaching (Institución Libre de Enseñanza, ILE). The brothers Juan and Venrua Alvarado toured rural areas recording observations about the surrounding villages, the living conditions of the pastoralist communities and the rich and diverse dairy culture in which they saw the main potential for rural empowerment (cheese being the millennia-old form of biotechnological storage for the summer pastures' protein surplus).

Guided by the idea of the *institucionalismo rural* as proclaimed by Francisco Sierra-Pambley, the Alvarados prepared a report whose recommendations and proposals remain relevant a century later. Propounding an integrated vision of the landscape in 'P' format—pastos, pastores, paisaje y paisanaje (pastures, pastoralists, the peasant landscape and its populace)—they emphasised the strategic importance of native livestock and indigenous breeds while propos-
5 ing a certain modernisation of traditional cheese-making processes. This has had a significant influence on the Shepherds' School project I started in 2004.

Another important initiative taken by the ILE included the so-called pedagogical missions, which were founded in 1931 to establish a number of travelling missions to train rural teachers and provide the population with educational and cultural activities such as lectures on the progress of health, hygiene and politics. For example, some cultural activities included theatre and puppet plays, listening to classical music on a gramophone, art exhibitions, and poetry and dancing soirées. As the Civil War and General Francisco Franco's dictatorship erased these programmes and their memory, at Inland we found it crucial to examine their legacy and reignite their spirit. This inspired the Inland project called Mobile Method, which mobilised crews of artists to (conversely) learn from rural communities, or more precisely, to co-learn by activating a series of artistic tools such as Carthologies, Mobile Kitchen, Radio Trashumante or Microarchitectures of Farming—a sort of collaborative hackathon taking a county as a unit of intervention.

Amongst these experimental educational projects that looked at rural reinvigoration and rural arts and crafts, today we need to re-think, or better said, to un-learn how contemporary art functions, and find out what needs to be changed at the core of arts education.

Inland launched in 2009 from a collaborative
5 agency I started in 2009, providing a platform for diverse actors involved in agricultural, social and cultural production. During its first stage (2010–2013) and taking Spain as an initial case study, Inland was engaged with artistic production in 22 villages across the country, including nationwide exhibitions and presentations and an international conference. This was followed by a period of reflection and evaluation, the launch of study groups about art and ecology, and a series of publications. Today, Inland functions as a collective focused on land-based collaborations and

economies as well as communities-of-practice as a substrate for post-contemporary art and cultural forms.

Inland has a radio station, an academy, produces shows, and it makes cheese. It is also a consultant for the European Commission on the use of art in rural development policies, while promoting the European Shepherds Network, a social movement to question those same policies. As of 2020, we have been coordinating the Confederacy of Villages, a network of art spaces across rural Europe.

Within this framework, different educational projects have been designed and implemented, targeting different age groups. We work with different schools and with the Museo Reina Sofia's education department in our Forest-Flock-Classroom, introducing our agroecology awareness programme to around 400 children per year. We also collaborate with the Spanish Commission for Refugees (CEAR) and other official institutions in Spain, offering activi-
5 ties for the children of refugee families. We have worked with rural youth in a project supported by the Ministry of Culture called 'Loud Voice', bringing spoken-word artists in to work with teenagers from different villages in order to reaffirm their rural identity. As part of our coordination of the World Alliance of Mobile Indigenous Pastoralists (WAMPI), we facilitate the participation of young nomads in the youth branch of the International Planning Committee for Food Sovereignty (IPC).

We also launched the Inland Academy (inland.org/academy) in 2020 to train young practitioners to develop their projects connecting art, ecology and social change. More than 200 postgraduate students have applied from all parts of the world.

Another important project that we have been supporting is the Shepherds' School (escueladepastores.es) which has existed since 2004 and aims to transmit knowledge related to mountain pastoralism and land custodianship. Around 100 people apply every year. We support the transition towards living on the land, and we develop cultural strategies to change the perception of what it means to have a form of life connected to the land.

This involves the safeguarding of seeds, animal breeds and knowledge crucial for an agroecological transition and for future generations not yet born. These components of resilient nourishing and biodiverse ecosystems have to be maintained for greater adaptability in times of climate crisis and uncertainty.

5 In many cases, the work we do is related to a future beyond our lifespan. We are recovering and reforesting an Atlantic Forest which is now a monoculture plantation of eucalyptus, working on improving soil conditions and multiplying bee populations. All these projects combine art, science, vernacular knowledge and social engagement.

A recent development of these ideas came from the *documenta 15* in Kassel in 2022 and the concept of the *lumbung* (a traditional Indonesian communal village barn) to define collective values, ways of governing the collective rice barn and projects that are to build the collective economy. As part of the latter, the *lumbung* created the Kios (Indonesian for kiosk) and Gallery, sustaining the different local ecosystems by rethinking the sales of merchandise and artwork. Alongside this, we developed both the *lumbung* land and *lumbung* currency, which are seen as projects that can build a *lumbung* value-based economy over the long term.

Since the launch of the working group *lumbung* land, we have realised the importance of looking at land-based projects and economies as a political commitment to rid art from its dependence on being a service sector activity funded by public or private investment. The vision involves a form of care for the land as a living support structure with which we co-exist. In this sense, the projects have in mind the agency of the land as a living aspect of the biosphere, and thus the need arises to aim our practices at uniting peasant and indigenous communities and becom-
5 ing custodians of the land to prevent extractivism and speculation. Organisations which have been working in this direction for many years and have started to exchange their practices and knowledge on these approaches include the Jatiwangi Art Factory, Wajukuu, Inland and Mas Arte Mas Accion.

The discussion has been focused on the collective governance of land and development models that start from community as well as on non-human needs, combining agriculture, biodiversity, human culture and the spiritual. Also, we think about how to see the 'investment' of the *lumbung* in specific pieces of the organisations' land. What would be the return, in financial and symbolic terms? Meanwhile, a land-discursive working group started to come into being. This group focuses on connecting the differing public programmes of *lumbung* collectives that look at reconnecting to the memory of the land and at how to build an imagery connected to the land which is based on artistic processes and indigenous poetry, songs and images in order to move beyond extractivist modernist uses. It also focuses on land restitution and what that means for ownership, the collective re-creation of narratives, and memories. These two groups became intertwined as learning processes.

Currently, we continue to look at the importance of the transfer and production of knowledge; we are discussing the possible form of a collective Lumbung Land School. The focus we chose for the proposed projects for this *lumbung interlokal* land project aligns with our vision of agroecology which has a holistic
5 approach and encompasses social, economic, environmental and cultural dimensions. This is not a school in the classic sense; rather, it is a container in which collective learning, harvesting and experimentation happens, the results being brought to the communal village barn, which also symbolises a depository of wisdom.

NATIONAL
GEOGRAPHIC

‘We are really fortunate to hold our sessions on the original BMC campus’

6

In autumn 2015, a group of creative thinkers gathered at the site of the former Black Mountain College
6 (BMC), the legendary school of free-thinking and
non-hierarchical learning that fostered the careers of
personalities like John Cage and Merce Cunning-
ham. They decided to set up a programme that would
tie in with the ideals of the historic school.

The School of the Alternative (SotA), an educational and community experiment, has existed since 2016 offering more opportunities to think, create and act together than other schools. Instead of traditional classes, the campus supports a collectively developed, self-directed learning approach that provides opportunities for all participants to learn and teach. Courses take place on the original Black Mountain College campus and are held each summer. They draw on the legacy of previous alternative schools and seek to set the stage for a modern community of pioneers, artists and critical thinkers.

COMMUNITY

Katja Klaus asked Heidi to answer her questions and share her thoughts …

Katja Klaus In a post on Instagram from May 11, 2023, you write, 'Nothing nourishes quite like living in a community where shared knowledge is a practice we all participate in.' What do you understand by a new community?

Heidi Gruner I think of a new kind of community as a
world-building space, one that collectively models the
6 sort of world we long for. A new community should be
imaginative, open, caring, adaptive. I want to use the
words of one of our other Board Members/facilitators
here, Maria Judice. She has spoken so beautifully of
the type of space we create, what our new community feels like.

'At SotA I can journey off into the unknown, find adventure, and wonder. In the everyday world, there is so much noise and fear, but in Black Mountain, I am encouraged to do my work—to gain my knowledge of self.

I return to SotA to attune my heart to the essential sounds. I know I am not alone. Every year I sit in silence with other participants while the trees, the wind, and the ancestors guide us. Returning is no small thing … I believe I am making a huge shift in the world simply by showing up. I am co-creating with a beautiful circle and making a world of my vision. This is the work. This is radical action. This is how my protest looks—building, revitalizing, restoring, and expanding thoughts and understanding.'

KK What community practices underpin your work, the vision of your school?

HG Thank you for asking this. From the beginning we have had a solid structure for our programming, our class types, what a day looks like, etc., but our community practices are where we have grown the most and into which we poured a lot of energy.

6 The way we host people is so crucial to this work. It's crucial to folks feeling safe here, to us limiting harm and to creating trust and solid community bonds. It's vital to creating a space where folks are free to explore and share. For us that means a lot of preventative practices and deep, intentional care while in session.

We have a community agreement: a living, breathing document that we read at the top of each week and that we send to folks prior to arrival. We encourage editing sessions where we look at the agreement together and make updates and changes to ensure that everyone feels considered within this agreement. These editing meetings have happened several times both during and between our sessions, both with our facilitators and with various participants. We also have a point person system at SotA: Leaders in the community cover a small group of folks (12 to 15), guiding them through orientation on the first night, and the group then has dinner together mid-week as a way of checking in. Point people are in continual communication with each other to ensure folks are cared for within our capacities. We added a really crucial position a few years ago, one we've been dreaming of for years. We now have an on-site mental health staff person, a licensed therapist, who is at our sessions to offer support if and when folks need it. We also have some protocols and processes for living in conflict and ways to work through those

moments with care for everyone involved, knowing
that conflict can be generative, too. We are really
6 continually nourishing this part of our work because
we know this is a huge part of our responsibility as
folks who are vocally offering a safe(r) space.

KK At which moments do you reach your personal limits in terms of community living?

HG I miss it so much when we're not in session. Community living feeds me (and all of us) in ways that I haven't been able to replicate in my day-to-day life. I think this is a huge advantage to our programming being just a few weeks every year: I really don't reach my limit. I leave wanting more. I can definitely feel closer to burning out if things have been especially intense or during years in which we had less on-site facilitators, but in reality, when we have a full team of folks on the ground helping tend the container, it honestly just feels good to be in our community the entire time, even when it's imperfect or hard.

PARTICIPANTS

KK What made you take on this task, the responsibility for this school?

HG My role at the school didn't start as director but as we grew, I took on more. I have a pretty high capacity for labour, and I saw the impact that the work was having on others and on myself. I do take on a lot of the logistical labour, but the school is really

upheld by all of us, everyone who attends. I have
both felt and seen the impact, and I continue with this
6 responsibility as long as I have this capacity because
I think it's important for spaces like this (of which
there are so many other than us) to exist.

This is work that feels important to me, my values, and the kind of world I want to help cultivate. It's hopeful. I need that, we need that to exist and help create spaces where we can have respite from a world that is continually trying to bring us down, to exist in a community free from traditional forms of hierarchy, individualism and competition. It is a needed balm.

I feel really grateful that my path has led me to this work. As hard as it can be, I also think that SotA can be a sort of container for hope and can help us see and shape not only this one experience we share, but our communities back home.

KK Who studies and who teaches at your school?

HG I hesitate to be too specific here, because really we hope for SotA to be a space that isn't just for one kind of person. Historically, this programming has appealed to folks who have felt restricted by traditional institutions and who want a space to explore educational ideas outside of academia. Folks who are curious and want to live collectively in a space that prioritises care.

Other than being over 18, there are no prerequisites
for studying or teaching at SotA. We are lucky to
6 have had a huge range of participants in terms of
place of origin, age, education, race, class, experience, and more. But our intentions are always to open our doors wider as we grow. Our recruitment work revolves around broadening the range of people who study and teach at SotA. Currently, the demographics of SotA skew towards white queer folks and people with higher-education, who live in large US cities. We hope to continue our journey towards radical accessibility by creating space for Black people and other people of colour as well as folks living in rural places. We fundraise towards making SotA more equitable and accessible by offering numerous scholarships, including our Black Equity Scholarships, and by being intentional about membership on our Board and Advisory Committee.

KK Have you had positive experiences with schools and learning in your life?

HD I've always worked best with projects that are self-directed or collaborative instead of steeped in hierarchy. I've had positive and negative experiences with schooling. I've had teachers who really encouraged and nourished my learning style and skillset, but I also really struggled in school overall. I got in trouble a lot, I talked a lot in class, I've never been super great with authority figures. I had a few professors in college who really encouraged me, and

I don't want to discount that, but overall I really struggled and was happy when it was over, to be honest.
6 I also have ADHD, and I always really struggled with how to adapt my learning style to a traditional classroom.

I think some of my best, generative times in traditional schooling were studio art classes in college. I studied graphic design, and being in the studio with the other folks in my programme, talking through each other's work and problem solving together was what aligned most with my growth as a student. Although critiques could be brutal. I think fear is used as a tool a lot in schooling, and the programme I was in required a review for entry a few years in, and that was really hard for me. My anxiety was through the roof, and I didn't have the tools to manage it. The traditional hierarchies in institutions were always really tough for me, and I pushed up against them to a degree that was probably prohibitive to my experience.

What drew me to this work is the opportunity to create a learning environment where space is made for all types of learners and where everyone's input helps shape the experience. This radical non-hierarchical setup has affected every aspect of my life outside of SotA, too.

I've always been a super curious person. I've always been a reader and a person who asks a lot of questions, and I am really amped up by the exciting prospect of being a lifelong learner. I think SotA has amplified this, too. One big lesson I have taken away from SotA is that there is just truly no value to re-

source hoarding or being a knowledge guardian. The
world is so competitive that I think a lot of folks tend
6 to hoard their knowledge, but the kind of world I want
to live in and the kind of world we try to enact at SotA
is one that values the great power in sharing what
you know.

LANDSCAPE

KK Can you describe the impact that the surrounding landscape has on your community and on your learning experience?

HD There is magic in this place. There is incredible history and beauty and palpable energy in Black Mountain, specifically on the campus that we inhabit; that's really hard for me to put into words. It's also nice that we're nestled in the woods, providing a sort of escape that I think is an appeal for a lot of people. The ability to tuck into the woods alone or with others is just something that you can't simulate. Perhaps most importantly, though, we're accessible to radical folks in the American South who want to attend programmes similar to ours but might not be in a place where they can travel extensively to get to one.

KK What happens on the site outside of your summer course?

HD The campus we are on is a YMCA event space, it actually has been since its inception, even when Black Mountain College was there—so they

were also renting space from the organisation we
rent space from. They have year-round conferences
6 and events from a variety of groups and host camps
in the summer. We meet every year in May because
it's their least busy time of year. We hope to always
be one of the few groups on campus when we're
there so we can really roam freely and use the entire
space, and maintain our container as much as
possible.

KK Under what conditions would it be conceivable for you to change to a year-round operation?

HD This really isn't doable for us and would really greatly exceed our capacity. Right now our programme is fully self-funded, meaning tuition (which we keep as low as possible) fully funds our essential needs, and any additional cost is sustained through small fundraising efforts. We would need major funding to buy land, pay ourselves a living wage, etc. And ultimately, I think SotA can still offer what we hope to offer with short sessions. So right now our focus is on keeping this project alive and nourishing its growth in other ways.

I've learned to frame growth outside of a capitalist mindset, and for us, growth means creating more access and sustainability. There are still so many folks who can't access our programming who want to (even with a full scholarship, getting money to travel here, time away from work and other obligations, etc., it is tough for so many). What would it look like for us

to get those folks here? What would that take? How
can our community and our facilitators feel supported
6 in this work so that it can sustain? Those are the big
growth questions swimming in my brain.

Ultimately I think this programme existing is more vital than this programme getting bigger. I also want to consider our internal collective and prioritizing space for rest and recharge alongside the sometimes grueling work of making this thing happen.

I do think it would be great to do a session in the fall as well as the spring. We've flirted with that, but the reality is we're just making it financially as is, and fundraising is hard (and newish) for us. Maybe one day! But beyond that, I don't think something like a year-round operation is our path.

SCHOOL/CURRICULUM

KK Is there any kind of curriculum for your school and the summer courses?

HD No, we don't have a set curriculum. We hope to respond directly to our community, to the collective community, so each year our curriculum looks different and is determined by the radical folks who apply to teach. We put out a call for applications each fall, and anyone can apply—there are no prerequisites or requirements. Then, a group from our community reviews the applications, and lastly, myself and my right-hand-person/co-creator/Board Member Nelle Dunlap will create a balanced curriculum from the top applicants' courses. Normally we work to

have a balance of things like making/thinking, intro-
spective content vs more playful content, etc. This
6 year, we had less ‘making’ applications and more
class proposals that aimed to hold space for process-
ing what’s happening in the world which looked like a
lot more writing this year and a lot less making. And I
think that’s what people needed at this time, so for us
keeping the call pretty open hopefully creates space
for us to meet the needs of the time by design.

KK Why did you change your school’s name from ‘Black Mountain School’ to ‘School of the Alternative'?

HD A larger institution had the rights for educational use of the phrase ‘black mountain’. We fought it, but lost. Our original founders were very tied to the name and really wanted to keep it. The inspiration that Black Mountain College offered to the inception of this project was important to them, which I understand. There was a silver lining to losing the name, though, and to be honest, maybe even a drop of relief. It was a lot to carry that weight, and in reality, while we are inspired by Black Mountain College and its legacy, we are doing our own thing; we are now responding to the very different needs of our present moment.

I also think we share that inspiration of BMC as an alternative learning space, it’s so far from unique to us. I think it’s probably safe to say (and very beautiful how) so many folks doing this kind of work are in-

spired by and pull from that legacy. So, although we
are on the original site and share much of the ethos, I
6 don't think we need the name. Our name is just one
piece of what we are, and it's nice to have something
that doesn't carry as much expectation. We are a
space that lives by alternative and radical ideas—one
of many.

KK What courses were offered this year?

HD Full class descriptions and faculty bios are on our website, but the lineup for this year's session was:
_Britt Billmeyer-Finn taught 'Instant Play'
_Dharushana Muthulingam taught 'Beyond the Hero's Journey: Storytelling to Make Sense of Care Work, Reckon with the Past, and Imagine Futures'
_Sabel Santa taught 'The Shadow and the Artist'
_Sophie Traub taught 'Re-re-re-Make—a Reiteration Workshop'
_Zoe Tuck taught 'Read Like a __________'
_Jonathan Curtin taught 'Queer Mobility Autonomy'
_Lo Bil taught 'Unexpected Arrivals: Joyful Performance Risks'
_Swati Piparsania taught 'Body as Site'

KK Are you in exchange with other international school experiments at home and abroad?

HD Yes, a bit, and we hope to do so more! Another facilitator of a similar programme (Sophie Traub

from The School of Making Thinking) taught a class
at SotA this year, and they and I were able to host a
6 pop-up event/radio show where we talked about run-
ning alternative art residencies. It was really inspiring to hear how they do things, to kind of chew on some things we were both thinking about together, and maybe mostly to share this with a large group, to demystify this work (we need more spaces like this!). That conversation has turned into another project, which is still in its infancy, where we are working to be in conversations with more facilitators and where we make those conversations accessible to others as an open resource. We're still figuring out what this will look like, but I think all of that is generative and hopeful and comforting, really, to speak with other folks doing this work. In 2016 we also attended an Alternative Art School fair at Pioneer Works in Brooklyn, and being with other facilitators there, albeit brief, was eye-opening. I wish I had 100 hours in a day to organise another gathering like that, this work can be grueling (but worth it, always), and it feels really vital to connect with others doing this, hopefully, transformative and world shifting work.

ALTERNATIVES

KK Which developments in the current education of artists and designers do you particularly dislike?

HD Those that don't consider varying identities and experiences or which value tradition over evolu-

tion. When an institution claims to hold space for varying identities but doesn't practice that in action.
6 Those that lack consideration of and deep care for folks holding identities that have historically been oppressed in institutions.

KK You promise 'spaces for a different logic, a new language, new categories of thought'. What alternatives do you specifically offer?

HD We hope to offer alternative class environments, where students impact the way the class is run as much as the faculty. It feels simple to say but huge and impactful to experience. I can alter the course of a class? My voice is as important as a faculty member's? That often opens up for folks the big beautiful idea that they can also teach what they know and are passionate about.

We vocally prioritise care and work to grow those practices. We create space for listening to our community about what they need from the school. For us in this work so far it's largely been about creating the conditions for folks to feel present and safe and engaged so that they are free to create, grow and thrive at SotA.

KK To what extent do academic discourses influence your work?

HD I'm not steeped in academic discourse really at all, to be honest. I think there are folks who are a

part of our community who are more interested in academia, and their resistance to certain aspects within
6 institutions I'm sure helps to shape our project, but my life outside of SotA is as an Art Director/Designer, and academia is not a part of my day to day. Where I am trying to learn and grow as a facilitator is more centred around radical world building and community care. Right now we really have to actively work to sustain this project alongside the rest of our lives and other work (SotA is volunteer-run), so what informs and influences this work most is our community and our in-person sessions. Are we meeting their needs? Are we meeting the needs of the communities we wish to serve?

LEGACY

KK In what way does the legacy of Black Mountain College still influence your work?

HD We likely wouldn't exist without the precedent, and so much of our foundation was built from their ethos. Non-hierarchical learning, work service/collective sustaining of the community, self-directed study, and so on. I feel really grateful for the ways that legacy was such a catalyst for this programme, but as a group we don't really refer to them the way we did at the start anymore. We are responding to such a different time. Sitting, always, in deep gratitude for the foundation, but/and growing from that original seed as we need to respond to the needs of our current world.

KK Do you see yourselves as the first official successor to Black Mountain College?

6

HD I don't. There are so many radical programmes that are doing work like this, and I would consider us a part of the collective of alternative art schools/residencies that carries on the legacy of programmes before us, like BMC. I think we are offering an alternative amidst a world that really needs more, just as they were offering an alternative in a world that really needed more. We are really fortunate to hold our sessions on the original BMC campus, and it really is powerful to be on that land, in their classrooms, dancing across the same lawn they danced across. So in that way we are connected, but I think it's more abstract than us being a successor.

An essay by Aleksandra Kędziorek

Reading time 14′

Opening the academy: Oskar Hansen's pedagogy of Open Form

In 1994, the classical courtyard of the Czapski Palace, the main seat of the Academy of Fine Arts in Warsaw, was filled with fabrics, birdhouses and sounds. Wide strips of grey canvas, spray-coloured and stretched between the buildings, created new spatial relations.

This way, the author of the installation, Oskar
7 Hansen, an architect and professor emeritus of the academy, intended to break the dictate of the Closed Form—he used this term to describe fully defined, dominant spaces that left no room for individual expression. The installation *To Trees and Birds*, designed in collaboration with Henryk Górka, introduced shapes that broke the pompous architectural style of the palace complex and the rigorously symmetrical rows of trees to bring out the richness of the existing life in the courtyard.

Stretched above people's heads, canvas strips emphasised individual trees and highlighted their diverse silhouettes, varied forms and textures of their trunks, and their mutual relations. A low-slung square with a cut-out circle framed the abundance of life on the lawn. The installation transformed the courtyard into a background for events—a non-hierarchical, absorptive space that Hansen called an Open Form.[1]

To Trees and Birds was not his only attempt to transform the Warsaw Academy of Fine Arts, both spatially and pedagogically. The architect, author of the Open Form theory and Polish member of the architects group Team 10, had been involved with the school since the 1950s when he returned from a schol-

arship in Paris. His Western experience—participation
in the CIAM Summer School in London and intern-
ships in the studios of Pierre Jeanneret and Fernand
Léger—was not appreciated during Stalinism. Thanks
to Jerzy Sołtan, former collaborator of Le Corbusier
and dean of the newly established Faculty of Interior
Design, he found refuge at the academy. He continued
7 his teaching activities for 30 years, first as an instructor
at the Solids and Planes Composition Studio (1955–
1970), then at the Visual Structures Studio (1971–
1981) at the Faculty of Sculpture. His classes on the
basics of visual composition were a continuation of a
prewar course run at the Warsaw academy by Wo-
jciech Jastrzębowski but had an original curriculum
based on the Open Form theory.

THE OPEN FORM

Developed since the 1950s and presented at the 1959 CIAM congress in Otterlo, the Open Form theory defined all areas of Hansen's activity.[2] In contrast to the Closed Form which included much of the architectural production to date—dogmatic, hierarchical, fully defined spaces that were mostly a monument to their designers—the Open Form introduced indeterminacy, flexibility, openness to changes, and the users' co-creation into the field of design.

The architecture designed in accordance with its principles was intended to provide a framework for life, act as a passepartout exposing the diversity of everyday events and foster human creativity. It was possible to adapt the theory to different disciplines and scales of design—from exhibitions and pavilions at trade fairs through housing estates designed together with Zofia Hansen, his wife and also an architect, to the Linear Continuous System, the concept of linear cities stretched throughout Poland—and it became Hansen's life philosophy and his way of describing the world around him.[3]

7 The theory also permeated his teaching practice. The experience of attending the Solids and Planes Composition Studio, compulsory for every student of the Faculty of Sculpture in the first years of their studies, was often recalled by the academy's graduates as being one of the ideologically strongest in their artistic education, even if they later chose to follow other paths. The curriculum[4] began with a series of compositional exercises based on dichotomies such as heavy and light objects, static and dynamic forms, and contrast of shapes and sizes. These were followed by exercises performed on didactic apparatuses—specially designed devices made from wood and plywood dedicated to studying the problems of 'rhythm', 'legibility of complex form' and 'Legibility of simultaneous movements'. Some of the exercises, including 'Combinatorics—a composition of one's own dwelling in a multi-story building' or 'legibility of large numbers of elements', directly addressed architectural problems under discussion at the time. For instance, the 'large number' referred to the concept of the 'greater number', which Hansen and the other members of Team 10 used as a way to address the problem of an ever-growing human population and its

impact on the built and natural environment. Another
exercise informed by ongoing debates, but unique in
its approach, was the 'active negative', a sculptural
interpretation of spatial sensations experienced by an
individual in an architectural interior. Developed in
1955 as a result of the remodeling of the Hansens'
own apartment, it corresponded to the global interest
7 in Gestalt psychology, but unlike the parallel studies
of negative space by Bruno Zevi or Luigi Moretti, it
was distinguished by the introduction of a subjective,
emotional factor.

A NON-HIERARCHICAL, OPEN-SYSTEM VS. A SYSTEM OF MASTER STUDIOS WITH THEIR UNIDIRECTIONAL KNOWLEDGE TRANSFER

In the 1970s, the curriculum of Hansen's studio was enriched by the introduction of open-air group exercises. They had begun outside of the academy as an initiative of young graduates and artists. In December 1971, Hansen participated in a meeting of the Young Creative Workshop in Elbląg where artist Przemysław Kwiek suggested moving the discussion outdoors and replacing words with visual communication—'a performed battle of "visual tactics"' that Hansen helped structure.[5] The resulting group action, known as *A Game on Morel's Hill*, inspired further exercises performed by Hansen and his students in open-air workshops in Skoki and Dłużew. There, students were encouraged to collectively construct an argument that questioned the hierarchy between author and audience or sender and recipient of a message—

each new voice picked up from where the previous one left off, composing a visual, open-ended dialogue.

In 1973, when the academy reclaimed its original premises on Wybrzeże Kościuszkowskie Street, the decision was made to use the building as the new seat of the Faculty of Sculpture. Hansen, the only architect employed at the faculty, was commissioned to
7 design its interiors. He intended to use this opportunity to create a suitable space for the pedagogy of the Open Form. A scheme from 1981 preserved in the collection of the Museum of the Academy of Fine Arts in Warsaw shows how far-reaching a change he proposed. Instead of the (partly still existing) system of master studios with their unidirectional knowledge transfer, rigid hierarchies and a finite list of tasks given to students, he advocated for a non-hierarchical, open system in which students could freely shape the programme of their own studies, determine their lengths, the way they worked (individually or in freely assembled teams) and the tasks they undertook. They would also summon professors only if they needed their help or advice, which would not only challenge established hierarchies but also clearly demonstrate students' sympathies and antipathies.[6] When he briefly held the office of dean, Hansen sought to establish the Open Form pedagogy as the official teaching method, but resigned from the position under pressure from other faculty members who did not like his pushing his own teaching ideas on a departmental scale.

The architect's involvement in teaching visual composition at the Faculty of Sculpture resulted in interesting transitions between disciplines. The Open Form, initially conceived as an architectural theory, became an inspiration for two generations of Polish artists who—also encouraged by Jerzy Jarnuszkiewicz, a professor who ran a parallel studio and introduced
7 photography to the teaching of sculpture—turned to performance and experimental film. Direct references and echoes of the Open Form can be found, for instance, in the oeuvre of Grzegorz Kowalski, Wiktor Gutt and Waldemar Raniszewski, KwieKulik (Zofia Kulik & Przemysław Kwiek) and in the work of Kowalski's students, including Paweł Althamer and Artur Żmijewski.[7]

Thanks to Svein Hatløy, a Norwegian architect who came to the Warsaw academy on a scholarship in the 1970s, the Open Form also found followers in architecture in Norway. The students at the Bergen School of Architecture, established by Hatløy in 1986, visited Hansen in his summer house in Szumin for summer schools in the 1990s.[8] The modest wooden house unintentionally became another teaching device to explain the principles of the Open Form. Filled with didactic apparatuses, it explained Hansen's assumptions through direct experience of them in the space. Now a monument and a branch of the Museum of Modern Art in Warsaw, it helps the next generation to understand Hansen's architectural thought, in line with his premise that 'philosophy is better promoted through space than through a philosophy book.'[9]

1 For more information on the *To Trees and Birds* installation, see Jola Gola (ed.), *Towards Open Form*. Frankfurt/Main: Revolver/Warsaw: Foksal Gallery Foundation, 2005, pp. 144–145. A video documentation is available in the film library of the Museum of Modern Art in Warsaw: https://artmuseum.pl/en/filmoteka/praca/hansen-oskar-
7 drzewom-i-ptakom-asp-warszawa-1994

2 This article focuses on his pedagogical practice. His vast architectural and artistic legacy was summarised in other publications, for instance Aleksandra Kędziorek and Łukasz Ronduda (eds.), *Oskar Hansen—Opening Modernism: On Open Form Architecture, Art and Didactics*. Warsaw: Museum of Modern Art, 2014; Łukasz Stanek (ed.), *Team 10 East: Revisionist Architecture in Real-Existing Modernism*. Warsaw: Museum of Modern Art, 2014; Jola Gola (ed.), *Towards Open Form*. Frankfurt/Main: Revolver/Warsaw: Foksal Gallery Foundation, 2005.

3 This approach is most evident in his book *Zobaczyć świat* (To see the world), modelled on Władysław Strzemiński's treatise *Teoria widzenia* (Theory of vision) (1957) that narrates the history of human creativity through the lens of Open Form and Closed Form. Oskar Hansen, *Zobaczyć świat*, edited by Jola Gola. Warsaw: Zachęta—Narodowa Galeria Sztuki, 2005.

4 A full curriculum is presented in Jola Gola, Grzegorz Kowalski (eds.), *30 years later: A look at Oskar Hansen's studio*. Warsaw: Academy of Fine Arts in Warsaw, 2013.

5 Łukasz Ronduda, Georg Schollhammer (eds.), *KwieKulik: Zofia Kulik & Przemysław Kwiek*. Warsaw: Museum of Modern Art/Wrocław: BWA Galleries of Contemporary Art/Vienna: Kontakt, 2012, p. 94; KwieKulik, *A Game on Morel's Hill (group action)*, 1971, film library at the Museum of

Modern Art in Warsaw, https://artmuseum.pl/en/filmoteka/praca/kwiekulik-gra-na-wzgorzu-morela-akcja-grupowa.

6 Filip Springer, *Zaczyn.* Kraków/Warsaw: Karakter, 2013, p. 211.

7 Their practices and their relation to Open Form are described in detail in Axel Wieder, Floryan Zeyfang (eds.), *Open Form. Space, Interaction, and the Tradition of Oskar Hansen.* Berlin: Stern-
7 berg Press, 2014; Łukasz Ronduda, 'In the circle of Open Form: Visual Games, Interactions, Participation, Archives, Communities', in: *Polish Art of the 70s.* Warsaw: CCA Ujazdowski Castle, 2009, pp. 171–201; Łukasz Ronduda, Michał Woliński, Axel J. Wieder, 'Games, Actions, Interactions: Film and the Tradition of Oskar Hansen's Open Form', in: Łukasz Ronduda, Floryan Zeyfang (eds.), *1, 2, 3 ... Avant-Gardes: Film/Art between Experiment and Archive.* Berlin: Sternberg Press/Warsaw: CCA Ujazdowski Castle, 2007, pp. 88–103.

8 A video documentation is available in the film library of the Museum of Modern Art in Warsaw: *Oskar Hansen. Summer School. Szumin 1991.* Muzeum Sztuki Nowoczesnej w Warszawie (artmuseum.pl).

9 Quoted after Filip Springer, *Zaczyn,* p. 5.

An essay by Lee Stickells

Reading time 15′

Ant Farm—Show/Blow Minds (Learn)

8

COWBOY NOMADS (OUTLAWS) SMOKE LOCO WEED AROUND ELECTRIC CAMPFIRES

The pop mediasphere (of which they were such insightful savants) best remembers the art group Ant Farm (1968–1978) for the ephemeral delights of their inflatable architecture experiments and for one of America's most familiar artworks, *Cadillac Ranch* (1974). Each generation rediscovers the squishy, floating, non-orthogonal fun of a do-it-yourself air-supported enclosure, while the ten Cadillacs, buried nose down in a tail-finned chorus line beside
8 iconic Route 66, continue to offer a loving critique of American car culture's pleasures and poisons.

'Genius practitioners of the carnivalesque' was Michael Sorkin's assessment, succinctly capturing Ant Farm's gonzo architectural reputation.[1] Felicity D. Scott pushes further, though, reading the experimental collective's work as 'a prescient instance of the discipline's encounter with, attempt to come to terms with, and critical engagement of an environment radically transformed by electronic media.'[2]

Ant Farm looked to do nothing less than reimagine architecture, responding to new electronic technologies, information networks, psychedelic drugs and a countercultural environmental consciousness being formed through encounters with the lexicon of an emergent planetary culture (from Marshall McLuhan's global village notion to NASA's 'blue planet' photographs). Their vision of future global media nomads 'smok[ing] loco weed around electric campfires' was at once a trippy riff on countercultural, tech-enabled communitarianism and a deadpan projection of architecture understood as interface, not shelter—mobile, multimedia, multichannel and core to a project of radical life reform. [3]

'EVERYTHING FROM EVERY DAY LIFE MUST BE MADE MAGIC' [4]

Ant Farm joined a number of young North American design communes emerging from the socio-cultural effervescence of the 1960s to challenge and remake what they decried as architectural pedagogy's stulti-
8 fying, technocratic framework. The context for their experiments was intense campus ferment, and the influence of a global 'anti-school', as Beatriz Colomina has put it, clustered around the thinking of figures such as Buckminster Fuller, Stewart Brand, Victor Papanek and Ivan Illich. [5]

Following Archigram's earlier lead, they styled themselves as countercultural rock groups with the mirrored sunglasses and names to match—Southcoast, Onyx, Pulsa, Zomeworks, Kamakazi Design Group, Space Cowboys, All Electric Medicine Show, etc. Largely through ephemeral, interactive, building-focused events ('build-in' workshops, 'moment villages', 'response environments') they looked to dissolve boundaries between students and teachers, and between work in the university and outside of it. [6] Architectural education was radically recast as an expanded site for situated learning, directly engaging with pressing environmental and socio-political challenges.

Ant Farm was launched by Chip Lord, Doug Michels and Curtis Schreier in the psychedelically auspicious year of 1968 and explicitly defined as a 'platform for educational reform'. One of their first actions was to disrupt the California Council of the A.I.A.'s annual convention with flyers questioning the profession's capacity to address the problems of 'the black ghetto, of the urban poor, of disoriented youth', and arguing the event's speakers be replaced with 'real trips, not instructive ones'.[7] Elsewhere, they directly infiltrated sites of architectural education. Projects such as *Astrodaze* and *Time Slice* (1969) at the University of
8 Houston were experiments in 'life art' that discarded conventional lectures for overnight beach happenings where 'everything from everyday life must be made magic', and camping in the city's Astrodome stadium, where students spent the night 'on and in a 60-foot parachute held aloft by helium balloons'.[8]

Non-hierarchical, freeform educational modes—echoing the radical prototypes of the recent free/anti-university movements—were key to Ant Farm's ambitions to dismantle the hierarchies and unidirectional information flow of architectural pedagogy. They also keyed into the countercultural refusal of the role played by the university in training compliant subjects for the military industrial complex.

Beyond infiltrating and remaking professional education, Ant Farm's pedagogical experiments were eventually marshalled towards establishing radically alternative modes of life. Resonating with the period's liberatory ideals, they pushed ideas of learning as a ‘continuous life process’ and the need to break from traditional pedagogical and professional institutions, spaces, and modalities.[9] An early example of the group’s acid-fuelled agitprop declared their purpose as: Show/blow minds (learn) environmental alternatives (urban-eco commune/high tech pneumads/pneu-family) [...] furthering super consciousness of clean ecological living + opening [sic] man/machine patterns to eco-consciousness: with open ended media systems and closed life support systems: how to live an eco-reality will [read: while] ‘truckin down the line’.[10]

Through their early educational experiments Ant
8 Farm began establishing a toolkit for this broader social and political agenda. Their ‘enviro-equipment’ embraced the conjugative possibilities of camper vans, video portapaks, poly film, industrial fans, LSD, the rock festival format and endless road tripping. Temporary events, creating counter-architectures in the gaps of America’s infrastructural networks, offered intense sensory experiences through ‘Dream-clouds’, ‘Rainbow Orchards’ and ‘Pink orifices’.

The more seriously utopian side to the spacy happenings of this hippie nomadology was a desire to deploy advanced technologies in everyday life, away from their dominant milieu and toward other ends. Ant Farm’s establishment of their ‘urban eco commune’ headquarters in Sausalito in late 1969 signaled an intensification of this agenda—the group gained more members, becoming ‘like a large commune’ and engaging with Northern California’s ecologically conscious, communitarian design counterculture.

'THE BERKELEY/ANT FARM/ MAD ENVIRONMENTALIST COALITION'

Ant Farm's visions of pedagogical transformation resonated with the prevailing countercultural orientation toward horizontal information networks and do-it-yourself education (promulgated most famously in the *Whole Earth Catalog*). Inflatables—the pneumatic structures Ant Farm referred to as 'pillows'—exemplified the group's architectural means for constructing the desired transformative mobility and interactivity.

For the counterculture, inflatables materialised qualities of ephemerality, flexibility and freedom, al-
8 lowed users to quickly shape their own environments, and offered an appropriate counter-form to conventional, 'square' architecture. As Caroline Maniaque notes, 'instead of the rigid walls associated with fixed behavior patterns, the supple surfaces promoted radically different behaviors—fluid, free, unexpected.'[11]

In support, Ant Farm's customised Chevrolet Media Van carried the required polyethylene films, adhesive tapes and tools to assemble the pillows and provided power to air pumps that inflated them. However, the Media Van was much more than just transportation. Blending influences from NASA's closed-system life support modules, American hot-rodding culture and military hardware, it was kitted out with extensive electronic equipment for audio, film and video recording and playback. It also towed the off-grid living unit 'Le Roy'—a trailer containing a kitchen, inflatable shower, solar collector and ICE 9 (a five-person inflatable Ant Farm lived in while on the road).

The Media Van, and the inflatables it could deploy, enabled Ant Farm to rapidly assemble its responsive educational environments for a new community of environmentally-conscious, cybernetically enhanced nomads.

The inflatables and the Media Van were documented in the *Inflatocookbook*, a do-it-yourself manual first published by the group in 1970.[12] The *Inflatocookbook* gathered evidence of Ant Farm's experiments to date as well as assembling and making the information and skills they'd learned accessible to an audience well beyond the architectural scene they
8 emerged from.

The book connected to pioneering alternative architecture manuals such as Steve Baer's *Dome Cookbook* (1968), Sim Van der Ryn's *Farallones Scrapbook* (1969), Lloyd Kahn's *Domebook* (1970) and even Stewart Brand's *Whole Earth Catalog* (1968–1972). *Inflatocookbook's* design and production also owed much to the methods of the countercultural media flourishing in North America. A bricolage of varied paper stock, stencils, typefaces, silkscreens, photo collages and cartoon illustrations, it offered step-by-step instructions in a humorous tone and invited readers' contributions to form a feedback loop.

The *Inflatocookbook* also outlined Truckstop Network, which offered the even more ambitious vision of a wholly dispersed alternative learning community: '[W]hat we are talking about is an institution, a communication network of places like ours, where media nomads can pull in off the road (earn College Credit!), repair a truck, video linkup throughout, tools of your trade, nutrients for every need.'[13]

Ant Farm's spring 1970 'Demonstration Tour' of schools, colleges, countercultural conferences and eco-activist interventions put the Truckstop Network idea into motion. It came at the high point of their inflatable period and centred on the *50 × 50' Pillow*—an inflatable commissioned for a failed rock concert in Japan.[14] Tour stops included the Earth People's park and the University of California's Sproul Plaza in Berkeley to stage their famous *Air Emergency* perfor-
8 mance for Earth Day (a pranksterish 'survival event' in which people were told that Ant Farm's pillow was the only safe space to escape deadly air failure). However, two other events in which they participated during the tour period clearly laid out the wider stakes for the group's educational experimentation.

First, in March 1970, Ant Farm participated in the Freestone Conference, at the invitation of its organiser, Berkeley architecture professor Sim Van der Ryn. Van der Ryn and his collaborators at the Farallones Institute had undertaken a series of architectural experiments in California public schools with progressive educators influenced by the free school movement. 'We are dominated by furniture', contended Van der Ryn and involved students in constructing inflatables and zonohedral structures that were simultaneously exercises in learning by doing and experiments in radically reconfiguring classroom space.

The Freestone gathering extrapolated in part from these efforts to break down rigid institutional spatial orders, emphasise non-hierarchical, collaborative design and an open-ended learning process. The goal, as Van der Ryn put it, was 'to learn to design new social forms, new building forms that are in harmony with life [...] to build a floating university around the design of our lives'.[15] Ant Farm's *50 × 50' Pillow* was an important contribution—a focal space for much of the event's activities.[16] Its significance for the Freestone community demonstrated that the inflatable (accompanied by the child-friendly *Inflatocookbook*)
8 had travelled well beyond the realm of rock concerts and avant-garde art interventions—it was comprehended as a more universal tool for establishing an alternative society.

In June 1970, again at the invitation of Van der Ryn, Ant Farm attended the International Design Conference in Aspen (IDCA), themed 'Environment by Design'. Here, they were part of a contingent of 'Environmental Action Groups' including Ecology Action, People's Architecture Group, Environment Workshop and Farallones Institute. Ant Farm arrived in their Media Van and, contrary to the organisers' proscriptions, set about assembling their *Spare Tire Inflatable*. The disruption did not end there.

The 'Berkeley/Ant Farm/Mad Environmentalist Coalition', as Reyner Banham disparagingly referred to them, were involved in a series of events that derailed conference proceedings. Non-programmed interventions (such as a chaotic name-badge swap

session) and a series of provocative proposed resolutions (criticising the IDCA's lack of real commitment to the environmental theme) highlighted ideological differences between the young counterculture radicals and venerable IDCA regulars. The environmental collectives and activist architects, with Ant Farm prominent among the voices, vigorously challenged any acceptance of designers as uncritical operatives within a capitalist, profit-driven system. They also demanded a more interactive, responsive conference format and a commitment to more authentic engagement with social and environmental concerns. It was
8 an ambitious attempt to re-educate the IDCA establishment.

Alice Twemlow has described the tumultuous conference and its aftermath in detail, showing that the IDCA board was, indeed, shaken by the events and experimented in subsequent conferences with more participatory formats.[17] The 'Berkeley/Ant Farm/Mad Environmentalist Coalition' contributed to reshaping the institution along countercultural lines. However, as Twemlow notes, the IDCA's embrace of these changes might be regarded 'as a textbook example of the capitalist system's ability to assimilate its own inherent contradictions, rather than resolving the real issues through definitive action'.[18]

Around 1971, Ant Farm's 'Truck stop fantasy one' bulletin would emphasise the group's conception of an open-ended pedagogy for an emerging post-institutional world—an education system as 'a continuous process with no finish with a degree and no start in "school".'[19]

It went on to ponder 'what happens when distinctions between gradeschool highschool college [sic] are removed? Incidental [sic] education for wandering learners little kids and old guys growing with mutual feedback.' Ant Farm's signaling here again of
8 education as a continuous, cybernetic process, outside the strictures and structures of traditional pedagogical institutions resonates with the counterculture's liberatory ideals and rhetoric. However, as Felicity Scott has soberly noted, the imagined freedom was in no way guaranteed.[20]

Open-ended, interactive forms of education and socialisation are all too smoothly deployed in what Gilles Deleuze termed a control society—training the nomadic subject of post-industrial culture in a requisite, continuous flexibility. To what extent Ant Farm recognised these ambiguities is open to question, making the revisiting of their propositions to reckon with the implications an endlessly valuable exercise.

1 Constance M. Lewellan and Steve Seid, *Ant Farm 1968–1978*. Berkeley: University of California Press, Berkeley Art Museum, Pacific Film Archive, 2004, p. 6.

2 Felicity D. Scott, *Living Archive 7: Ant Farm*. New York: ACTAR, 2008, p. 9.

3 *Ant Farm*, 'The Cowboy from Ant Farm (Cowboy Nomad Manifesto)', 1969. Ant Farm Archive, University of California, Berkeley Art Museum, Pacific Film Archive.

4 ANT FARM, TIME SLICE assignment handout, 1968, quoted in Scott, *Living Archive 7*, p. 45.

5 Valerio Borgonuovo and Silvia Franceschini (eds.), *Global tools: when education coincides with life, 1973–1975.* Rome: NERO, 2018, p. 5.

6 C. Ray Smith, *Supermannerism.* New York: E.P. Dutton, 1977, p. 25.

7 Scott, *Living Archive 7*, pp. 38–40.

8 'An Astrocamp?' *The Houston Chronicle* (article reproduced in Ant Farm Timeline, Scott, *Living Archive 7*, p. 208).

9 Doug Michels and Robert Field, Contribution to
8 'What's Wrong with Architectural Education?', *Architectural Forum* (July/August 1968), pp. 56–57. Michels and Field took the opportunity to discuss 'general notions about the learning process and the current situation in this country' in their article.

10 Ant Farm, *Intents & Purposes* (Truckstop Network Proposals folder), 1970. Ant Farm Archive.

11 Caroline Maniaque, 'Searching for Energy', in: Lewellan and Seid, *Ant Farm*, p. 17.

12 After selling out, a second edition of the *Inflatocookbook* was published in 1971 by Rip Off Press, the underground comics publisher.

13 *Inflatocookbook.*

14 Interview with Ant Farm (Constance M. Lewallen in conversation with Chip Lord, Doug Michels, and Curtis Shreier), in: Lewallen and Seid, *Ant Farm*, pp. 47–48.

15 Sim Van der Ryn, quoted in Forrest Wilson, 'Editorial', *Progressive Architecture* (July 1970), p. 70.

16 Sim Van der Ryn, *Farallones Scrapbook.* New York: Random House, 1972, p. 27.

17 Alice Twemlow, 'I can't talk to you if you say that: An ideological collision at the International De-

sign Conference at Aspen, 1970', *Design and Culture*, 1:1 (2009), pp. 23–50. See also Martin Beck, *The Aspen Complex*. London: Sternberg Press, 2012.

18 Twemlow, 'I can't talk to you', p. 43.

19 'Truck stop fantasy one', single typescript page, c. 1971, Ant Farm Archive, reproduced in Scott, *Living Archive 7*, p. 104.

20 Scott, *Living Archive 7*, pp. 105–109.

KATJA KLAUS

p. 49 Katja Klaus is a research associate at the Academy of the Bauhaus Dessau Foundation, acting as deputy head of the department since 2018. Her work focuses on pedagogy, design and digital mediation. After obtaining a certificate of advanced studies as Digital Curator from Pausanio Academy, Cologne, in 2021, she has been responsible for the digital research project *Schools of Departure*, an online atlas of design and art education beyond the Bauhaus. Furthermore, since 2020 Katja has been in charge of developing online teaching modules in the context of the international Bauhaus Open Studios programme, which she has been heading since 2015, and the online programme *Vorkurs Module*. From 2005 to 2014, the media, theatre and pedagogy scholar (MA) was an advisor to the director of the Bauhaus Dessau Foundation.

GREG CASTILLO

p. 59 Greg Castillo is a professor of architectural history at the University of California at Berkeley with research interests in 20th-century building cultures. He was the guest curator for the installation of *Hippie Modernism: The Search for Utopia* at
9 the Berkeley Art Museum and Pacific Film Archive and a contributor to the exhibition catalogue. His current research examines the legacy of the San Francisco Bay Area as a cradle of alternative design and building practices and the role of the 20th-century American model home as a prototyping instrument for speculative material cultures and lifestyles.

BINNA CHOI

p. 71 Binna Choi is a curator, writer and organiser. She's currently the curator of the Hawai'i Triennial 2025. From 2008 to 2023, she served as the director of the Casco Art Institute: Working for the Commons in Utrecht, the Netherlands. Under her directorship, Casco explored the commons as an alternative to binary worldviews and systems through and for art, taking that view as their organising guideline. Her key curatorial-collaborative projects at Casco include *Grand Domestic Revolution* (2009–2012), *Site for Unlearning (Art Organization)* (2014–2018), *Travelling Farm Museum of Forgotten Skills* (2018–ongoing) alongside engagement with networks like Arts Collaboratory and Cluster. Choi served as artistic co-director of the

Singapore Biennale 2022, *Natasha*, and she was the curator for the 11th Gwangju Biennale, titled *The Eighth Climate (What does art do?)*. As a member of Academy of the Arts of the World in Cologne, Germany, she curated the exhibition project *Gwangju Lessons* (2020), which travelled to the Asia Culture Center in Gwangju, South Korea. Choi is also a member of the faculty of the Dutch Art Institute and an advisor for Afield, which calls itself 'an international network of cultural change-makers'.

ANDRÉS GARCÉS ALZAMORA WITH KATHERINE EXSS CID, DAVID LUZA CORNEJO, RODRIGO SAAVEDRA VENEGAS

p. 84 Andrés Garcés Alzamora is a Doctor of Architecture with 29 years of professional architectural and teaching practice. He is a professor at the School of Architecture and Design at the Pontificia Universidad Católica de Valparaíso (PUCV) in Chile and a member (since 1994) and former president of the Corporación Cultural Amereida—Ciudad Abierta (Amereida Cultural Corporation—Open City). He was previously head of the Department of Architecture and Urbanism Projects of the PUCV's School of Architecture and Design where he was in charge of
9 large-scale projects contributing to the development of public assets in Chile. Katherine Exss Cid is a designer from the School of Architecture and Design (EAD) at the Pontificia Universidad Católica de Valparaíso. She received her Master of Arts degree in Information Design from the University of Reading, UK, and now is a PhD candidate in Architecture and Urbanism at the Universidad del Bío Bío, Chile. Currently she is on a research visit to UC Berkeley, USA. David Luza Cornejo is an architect from the Pontifical Catholic University of Valparaíso. He has gained a doctorate in Architecture from the Universitat Politècnica de Catalunya Barcelona. The title of his thesis from 2013 is *The constitution of the common extension of the Open City*. He is a professor at the School of Architecture and Design of the PUCV. Since 2022, he has been Director of the Observatorio Regional de Desarrollo Urbano Sostenible (Regional observatory for sustainable urban development) of the same university. Rodrigo Saavedra Venegas is a tenured professor at the School of Architecture and Design of the Pontificia Universidad Católica de Valparaíso, from which he himself gradu-

ated as an architect. He gained his doctorate from the Universitat Politècnica de Catalunya Barcelona in Spain with a thesis written in the framework of the Architectural Projects Programme of the Escola Tècnica Superior d'Arquitectura de Barcelona.

FERNANDO GARCIA DORY

P. 91 Fernando Garcia Dory is an artist, shepherd and agroecologist living between Madrid, Mallorca and Northern Spanish mountains. He brings together art and agroecology to provide alternative strategies for ecological action and rural revitalisation. During its first stage (2010–2013) and taking Spain as an initial case study, Inland was engaged with artistic production in twenty-two villages across the country, nationwide exhibitions and presentations, and an international conference. This was followed by a period of reflection and evaluation, launching study groups on art and ecology, and a series of publications. Today Inland promotes land-based collaborations and economies, and communities-of-practice as a substrate for post-contemporary art and cultural forms.

HEIDI GRUNER

9 p. 103 Heidi Gruner is a dynamic and enthusiastic creative professional who works to foster spaces of inevitable connection through enduring and thoughtful work. She has worked as a gallery director, graphic designer, art director and organiser. She has served on the board of the School of the Alternative (SotA) since 2016 and currently serves as the school's Executive Director. At SotA, she is committed to hosting an equitable space of communal learning and collective care, and to continually expanding and nourishing the ways we do both.

ALEKSANDRA KĘDZIOREK

p. 121 Aleksandra Kędziorek is an architecture historian, curator and editor based in Warsaw. She has curated exhibitions on modern architecture and design including *The Clothed Home: Tuning in to the Seasonal Imagination* (London Design Biennale, National Museum in Krakow, Lisbon Architecture Triennale, 2021–2022) and *Oskar Hansen: Open Form* (MACBA in Barcelona, Serralves Museum in Porto, Yale School of Architecture, Museum of Modern Art in Warsaw and National Gallery in Vilnius, 2014–2017). She also served as a curator of the Oskar and Zofia Hansen House in Szumin (2013–2017) and is the co-editor of *CIAM Archipelago: The Letters by Helena Syrkus* (with Katarzyna Uchowicz and Maja Wirkus, 2019) and *Oskar Hansen—Opening Modernism: On Open Form Architecture, Art and Didactics* (with Łukasz Ronduda, 2014). She is currently affiliated with the Museum of Warsaw.

LEE STICKELLS

p. 131 Lee Stickells is Head of Architecture at the University of Sydney. His historical research on international countercultural and ecological design experimentation has been published widely across scholarly, professional and popular media. He is actively engaged in creative and curatorial practice—collaborating with organisations such as the Museum of Contemporary Art, Sydney, the Christchurch Art Gallery and the Lismore Regional Gallery. He serves on the editorial committee of the *Architectural Theory Review*, the International Advisory Board for *Counterculture Studies* and the steering group of the Counterculture History Coalition. Whenever he gets the chance, he can be found riding a bike.

9

IMAGE CREDITS

p. 48 Bauhauslers on the terrace in front of the canteen (below, standing from right: Selman Selmanagic, Jean Weinfeld, Hilde Reiss) Bauhaus Dessau Foundation (I 6507 F) / © (E. Pius Pahl) Peter Jan Pahl.

p. 58 Berkeley's 'Outlaw Builders' constructing The Ark, a combination drafting room, dining hall and commons area. Photo: Jim Campe, Jim Campe document collection, Environmental Design Archives, University of California, Berkeley. p. 8.

p. 70 A knife inscribed 'I love you in the name of the commons', a farewell gift from Yolande Zola Zoli van der Heide to the Casco team, in the hands of Yolande and Binna Choi. 2019. Photo: Binna Choi.

p. 82 *The Courtship Tournament*, Jose Vial Amstrong historical archive.

p. 90 Little Museum of the Commons, intervention at the village of Almonaster La Real, with artist Susabna Velasco and neighbours, 2011. Courtesy of Inland.

9 p. 102 Jonathan Curtin leading her class 'Queer Automative Theory'. Photo: Lauren Panichelli.

p. 120 Students performing the 'Rhythm' exercise. Museum of Warsaw Academy of Fine Arts.

p. 130 Ant Farm's *50 × 50' Pillow* installed at the Freestone Conference, 20–22 March 1970. Photo: Jim Campe; courtesy of Jim Campe.

SCHOOLS OF DEPARTURE

#1 Decolonising design education
#2 The New Designer: Design as a profession
#3 Experiment: Learning communities
All issues can be found under:
atlas.bauhaus-dessau.de/en/journal

IMPRINT

The *Schools of Departure* series is published in connection with the online research platform of the same name, a digital atlas established by the Bauhaus Dessau Foundation with the objective of mapping experiments in art and design education beyond the Bauhaus. These experiments are understood as manifestations of travelling concepts which, with ever-shifting connotations, keep a wide variety of educational approaches in a process of constant exchange and motion. Studying these phenomena through the lens of travelling concepts such as Decolonisation, New Designers, New Communities, Creativity, Craft, Science, or Deschooling enables us to explore narratives around 'routes of appropriation' that move between different geographies, times and cultures.

This book assembles a selection of texts that were initially created for the online research platform in late 2022. It is one of three inaugural issues of the series, with new volumes to appear on a yearly basis.

The online research platform *Schools of Departure* was partly funded in 2021 in the context of the Digital Agenda for the State of Saxony-Anhalt with funds from the Ministry of Infrastructure and Digital Affairs of the State of Saxony-Anhalt. In 2022, the project has been further developed as part of *dive in. Programme for Digital Interactions* of the Kulturstiftung des Bundes (German Federal Cultural Foundation) with funding by the Federal Government Commissioner for Culture and the Media (BKM) through the NEUSTART KULTUR programme.

atlas.bauhaus-dessau.de

Bauhaus Dessau Foundation
Gropiusallee 38
06846 Dessau-Roßlau
Germany
represented by:
Director and CEO
Barbara Steiner

Edited by
Katja Klaus

Proofreading
Petra Frese, Frederik Richthofen

Design
Yvonne Tenschert, based on a concept by Offshore (Isabel Seiffert and Christoph Miler)

Coding
Leonardo Angelucci, 0x000.ch

Printing and Binding
Westermann Druck Zwickau GmbH

Publisher
Spector Books
Harkortstraße 10, 04107 Leipzig
www.spectorbooks.com

Distribution
Germany, Austria: GVA, Gemeinsame Verlagsauslieferung Göttingen GmbH & Co. KG, www.gva-verlage.de
Switzerland: AVA Verlagsauslieferung AG, www.ava.ch
France, Belgium: Interart Paris, www.interart.fr
UK: Central Books Ltd, www.centralbooks.com
USA, Canada, Central and South America, Africa: ARTBOOK/ D.A.P., www.artbook.com
South Korea: The Book Society, www.thebooksociety.org
Japan: twelvebooks, www.twelve-books.com
Australia, New Zealand: Perimeter Distribution, www.perimeterdistribution.com

First Edition, 2025
Printed in Germany

ISBN 978-3-95905-830-8

The Bauhaus Dessau Foundation is a non-profit foundation under public law. It is institutionally funded by:

Der Beauftragte der Bundesregierung für Kultur und Medien

Dessau
Roßlau